MW01716808

The Remnant

THE REMNANT

Shine International

The Remnant

Copyright © 2026 Shine International
First edition May 2026
Published by Shine International
Phoenix, Arizona
Email: shinebooksmedia@gmail.com
Website: www.shineinternational.org

ISBN 978-1-962580-10-6

All rights reserved. No part of this publication may be reproduced or transmitted in any form or by any means, electronic or mechanical, including photocopy, recording, or any information storage and retrieval system, without permission in writing from the copyright owner.

All Scripture quotations, unless otherwise indicated, are taken from the Holy Bible, New King James Version. Copyright ©1982 by Thomas Nelson, Inc. Used by permission. All rights reserved.

Those from among you
Shall build the old waste places;
You shall raise up the foundations of many generations;
And you shall be called the Repairer of the Breach,
The Restorer of Streets to Dwell In.

Isaiah 58:12

CONTENTS

INTRODUCTION

In this book we will study the topic of the remnant. It is an important theme, and it is highlighted throughout Scripture, even when the term itself is not explicitly used. Nevertheless, the word does appear in various parts of Scripture, especially in the prophetic books, as we will see in this study.

We will begin this study by looking at God's story with man since the Fall.

God's Story With Man Since the Fall

Since the Fall of Man, the Lord has revealed the plan of redemption:

The seed of the woman shall bruise the head of the serpent.

This is a familiar phrase taken from Genesis 3:15, in which God proclaims His final verdict after speaking with Adam, Eve, and the serpent, saying:

> *And I will put enmity between you and the woman, and between your seed and her Seed; He shall bruise your head, and you shall bruise His heel* (Genesis 3:15).

Since that time, the Lord had patiently and eagerly, with amazing love for humanity, been observing and waiting for this Seed, or Descendant, to come. Throughout the generations, He had been seeking those who would work with Him towards the fulfilment of this purpose until the time came when this awaited Descendant was prepared. These are the ones who worked with God in preparation for the Seed's coming.

The first person who brought comfort to God's heart was Enoch.

- **Enoch**

His name means 'dedicated' or 'consecrated'. Through the example of Enoch's life, God revealed to us what it means to live a truly consecrated life for the Lord. The secret of such a life is to walk with God. In Genesis 5:24, we read: *'And **Enoch walked with God**; and he was not, for God took him'*.

This shows that true consecration to the Lord is a walk—a dynamic movement of the spirit, a walk with God. Consequently, there must be specific matters pertaining to God's Kingdom that are accomplished according to God's plan.

God does not walk randomly or aimlessly with those who are consecrated to Him. Therefore, it is not possible for someone to walk with God and yet his life and days remain barren—without fruit or without the fulfilment of the matters which the Lord desires to accomplish through those who walk with Him.

It is therefore evident that God Himself accomplishes these purposes in fellowship with the consecrated; yet it is necessary that man, to whom the earth was given, be found and made available to God.

God desires for man to partake in the work because He has given man the responsibility over the earth; He entrusted the earth to him. This is clearly stated in Psalm 115: *'The heaven, even the heavens, are the Lord's; but the earth He has given to the children of men'* (Psalm 115:16).

"Where is my land? Where is my responsibility?" Every consecrated person must ask himself these questions.

The more one thinks in this way, the more steadfast and established his fellowship with God becomes. The Lord looks upon such a heart and says, "This is My servant whom I will entrust." Consequently, He reveals His will to him.

This is what truly makes life meaningful. Man was created for a purpose; therefore, he must discover the reason for which he was created, for this is what gives meaning to his life. If he does not, there will always be an inner groaning that surfaces from time to time, asking, "What am I living for?"

- **Noah**

After Enoch, God found Noah. Evil increased, and the Lord decreed the following concerning the earth and all that was in it because of the great wickedness:

> *Then the Lord saw that the wickedness of man was great in the earth, and that every intent of the thoughts of his heart was only evil continually. And the Lord was sorry that He had made man on the earth, and He was grieved in His heart. So the Lord said, "I will destroy man whom I have created from the face of the earth, both man and beast, creeping thing and birds of the air, for I am sorry that I have made them"* (Genesis 6:5–7).

Here we ponder: Does this mean that God ended the existence of humanity and creation and that the earth would return to its original state before creation?

The answer is "No", for God has an amazing and wondrous mystery which we need to understand. In accordance with this mystery, the divine timings are set.

The mystery is that the Lord waits to find those whom He will preserve amid this great judgement, so that through them the human race may continue and God's purposes may be fulfilled. This person must be different from all the rest, be separate from the wickedness around him, and live according to God's commandments and righteousness—meaning that he must live in the uprightness that is revealed in his heart through an inner divine mystical work.

At the time when He finds such a person, the divine timings are completed, the time of judgement is manifested, and the person preserved to accomplish God's will is made known.

This is exactly what happened before the Flood, as we read in the verse that follows, verse 8: *'But Noah found grace in the eyes of the Lord'*.

This is the kind of man who can bring comfort to God's heart, which is wounded as a result of man's wickedness. In fact, this is the meaning of his name, as we read in Genesis 5 about the name given to him by his father and the reason he was given it:

> *Lamech lived one hundred and eighty-two years, and had a son. And he called his name Noah, saying, "**This one will comfort us** concerning our work and the toil of our hands, because of the ground which the Lord has cursed"* (Genesis 5:28, 29).

Here we see how the curse that came upon the earth as a result of man's sins—through Adam, who fell, and through his son Cain, who killed his brother—not only caused pain and a wound in God's heart, but also brought pain and weariness to man himself: *'our work and the toil of our hands'*. These words indicate that the work had been hard and the yield small, thus leaving pain in the heart of man himself as well.

Now, let us look at what was said about Noah in order to understand more about how he lived and why he was chosen:

> *Noah walked with God* (Genesis 6:9).

Again, we see the importance of walking with God—that is, living a dynamic life that allows the Lord to work with a person, so that the achievements of God's Kingdom, according to His plan and timing, may be revealed.

In Genesis 7:1, we learn more about Noah:

> *Then the Lord said to Noah, "Come into the ark, you and all your household, because I have seen that you are righteous before Me in this generation."*

God looked upon an entire generation and found one person with whom He could work. This brought joy to His heart. How much more it would please Him if He were to find more than one!

God testified that Noah was righteous, meaning that he was upright in both heart and conduct. Noah continued to build the ark for about a hundred years (compare Genesis 5:32 and Genesis 7:6). It is obvious that during that time, he was exposed to a great deal of mockery and disapproval from those around him.

Nevertheless, he continued his work of building the ark, and thus he became a witness—or rather, a condemnation—to his generation, as mentioned in the Epistle to the Hebrews:

> *By faith Noah, being divinely warned of things not yet seen, moved with godly fear, prepared an ark for the saving of his household,* ***by which he condemned the world and became heir of the righteousness*** *which is according to faith* (Hebrews 11:7).

This means that God will bring that generation before Him and say, "Did not Noah live among you?" Thus, Noah will stand as a testimony against his generation; he will condemn them.

In the same way, every person who truly walks with God becomes a testimony—and even a condemnation—to his generation.

Noah was also a man of a covenant with God, as we read in Genesis 6:18, 19:

> *But I will establish My covenant with you; and you shall go into the ark—you, your sons, your wife, and your sons' wives with*

> *you. And of every living thing of all flesh you shall bring two of every sort into the ark,* ***to keep them alive with you****; they shall be male and female.*

The phrase *'to keep them alive with you'* draws our attention.

God preserved the human race so that it might continue according to His plan, despite what the enemy had done and despite man's disobedience and sin.

God found a righteous man and established a covenant with him because, through him, the human race would continue and God's plan would continue towards its intended purpose, as we shall see later.

The Flood ended, and Noah and his family came out of the ark to begin a new phase. It was a new beginning; therefore, God gave Noah the same blessing He had first given to Adam:

> *So God blessed Noah and his sons, and said to them: "Be fruitful and multiply, and fill the earth"* (Genesis 9:1).[1]

Yet, unfortunately, Noah could not impart to his children the type of life he lived: living in righteousness, in the covenant with God, and with the understanding of God's ways that had been revealed up to that time.

A side comment:

This is a sad and stumbling situation: a godly father who understands God's will, yet is unable to impart it to his children!

It is truly unfortunate, because it is the parents' responsibility. They often care for their children's physical and material needs, yet fail to focus on the purpose for which their children live.

1 Compare this with Genesis 1:28.

It is the parents' duty to help their children live out the same faith that they themselves practice.

Let us see what the Lord says about this responsibility:

> *Hear, O Israel: The Lord our God, the Lord is one! You shall love the Lord your God with all your heart, with all your soul, and with all your strength. And these words which I command you today shall be in your heart.* ***You shall teach them diligently to your children****, and shall talk of them when you sit in your house, when you walk by the way, when you lie down, and when you rise up. You shall bind them as a sign on your hand, and they shall be as frontlets between your eyes. You shall write them on the doorposts of your house and on your gates* (Deuteronomy 6:4–9).

Here the Lord says that parents should teach their children and speak with them about God's commandments and statutes, so that they sleep and rise with nothing more important in their lives than God's Word.

Unfortunately, when parents began to study psychology, they started saying, "We now understand that we need to teach them these matters gradually, so that they do not reject this spiritual path altogether."

Thus, we find examples of evil among Noah's descendants who spread throughout the earth at that time (Genesis 10). For example, we read about Nimrod, one of these evildoing descendants:

> *Cush begot Nimrod; he began to be a mighty one on the earth.* ***He was a mighty hunter before the Lord****; therefore it is said, "Like Nimrod the mighty hunter before the Lord." And* ***the beginning of his kingdom was Babel****, Erech, Accad, and Calneh, in the land of Shinar* (Genesis 10:8–10).

According to the original Hebrew text, the phrase *'before the Lord'* means *'against the Lord'*. Yet again, man began to turn away from obeying God, and even resist God. Man chose to listen more to Satan—the enemy of both humans and God—than to listen to and obey God. Thus, man began to establish a kingdom for himself, demonstrating independence from God's plans. This marked the beginning of Babel, from which all evil emerged.

Moreover, in the following chapter, we see how humans came together to carry out a plan that was clearly against God: building the Tower of Babel in the land of Shinar—the same land which Nimrod had established. Here we see the spread of Nimrod's evil and the formation of a group of people who devised a plan against God. In response, the Lord confused their language. Up until this point, they had all spoken one single language. What a great loss—for thenceforth man could no longer communicate with his fellow human, as their language became different, and language is an expression of both mind and heart!

How deeply saddening this must have been for God's heart!

God was continuing to observe the direction towards the emergence of the awaited Descendant, the one who was to bruise the head of the serpent. At the same time, the enemy was continuing to actively and cunningly work in the opposite direction, seeking to divert humanity from God's path.

The Lord waited patiently and steadfastly. Then, He found a man who could walk with Him so that God would continue the journey towards the coming of the awaited Descendant. This man was Abraham.

- **Abraham**

The prophet Isaiah speaks of Abraham, saying:

> *Look to Abraham your father, and to Sarah who bore you; for I called him alone, and* ***blessed him and increased him*** (Isaiah 51:2).

This was another new beginning after the events of the Tower of Babel:

The Lord found Abraham and gave him the same blessing He had first given to Adam[2]—*'blessed him and increased him'*.

After the events of the Tower of Babel, we read:

> *Now the Lord had said to Abram: "Get out of your country, from your family and from your father's house, to a land that I will show you. I will make you a great nation; I will bless you and make your name great; and you shall be a blessing. I will bless those who bless you, and I will curse him who curses you; and in you all the families of the earth shall be blessed."* ***So Abram departed as the Lord had spoken to him,*** *and Lot went with him. And Abram was seventy-five years old when he departed from Haran* (Genesis 12:1–4).

Abraham obeyed, and the Lord was with him.

Isaac, his son, was born miraculously in his father's old age. Isaac begot Jacob, and Jacob begot twelve sons, who became the nucleus of a people later called God's people—Israel.

Amid this journey, from Abraham to Israel, we notice:

- A foreign descendant appeared: Ishmael.

We find that God allowed this line to extend for some time, then He turned His gaze away from it. In Genesis 36, the account of

---

2 See Genesis 1:28

Ishmael's descendants comes to an end, just as in Genesis 4, when God turned His gaze away from Cain and his descendants.

[This is a very serious and dangerous matter that we must heed. A person may be walking with God, but if he pursues his own plans instead of God's, the Lord will withdraw and work with others—those who are truly His men. As a result, such a person will find that everything in his spiritual life collapses.]

God thus continued to focus on the line of descent from which He expected the awaited Descendant, who would bruise the serpent's head, to come.

- We notice another point in this journey from Abraham to Israel, highlighted in Genesis 38—a chapter which appears to be inserted in the middle of the story of Joseph, the son of Jacob.

This chapter speaks about Judah, the tribe from which the awaited Messiah was to come. We see that Judah deviates to strange matters. Then, the account takes us back to the rest of Joseph's life in Genesis 39.

It is thus clear that the Spirit of God works steadily and consistently with those who obey God towards the required purpose. At the same time, the evil one works cunningly and wickedly to divert this walk, seeking to hinder God's purposes, which he greatly fears.

- The third remark concerns a phrase we might easily overlook—the words which Joseph spoke to his brothers after he became ruler in Egypt.

When his brothers recognised him, they were afraid that he might take revenge because they had sold him as a slave to the Ishmaelites, who then brought him to Egypt.

However, God's plan for Joseph was manifested, as He turned their evil act into a preparation for the great task that awaited Joseph, as we read in the Psalm:

> *He sent a man before them—Joseph—who was sold as a slave. They hurt his feet with fetters, he was laid in irons. Until the time that his word came to pass, the word of the Lord tested him. The king sent and released him, the ruler of the people let him go free. He made him lord of his house, and ruler of all his possessions, to bind his princes at his pleasure, and teach his elders wisdom* (Psalm 105:17–22).

Joseph understood this about what had happened to him, and because he was righteous and walked with God, he did not hold a grudge against his brothers. Rather, he was enlightened by the Spirit of God and understood God's plan. Therefore, he said to his brothers:

> *But as for you, you meant evil against me; but God meant it for good, in order to bring it about as it is this day, to save many people alive* (Genesis 50:20).

Earlier, he had said to them:

> *And God sent me before you all* ***to preserve for you a remnant in the land*** *and to keep alive among you many survivors* (Genesis 45:7, LEB).

Let us reflect on this important phrase that Joseph had said to his brothers—*'to preserve for you a remnant in the land'*:

There had been a great famine in Egypt lasting seven years. It was expected that this famine would destroy an entire nation, causing everyone to perish. Yet, we find that God, who is wondrous in His ways, intervened and orchestrated several matters together, directing them towards the fulfilment of His purposes:

- Though He allowed the evil act of Joseph's brothers to happen, since He does not interfere with man's free choice, He turned their evil into part of His plan to prepare this man of God so that He could use him to fulfil His purposes.
- He was with Joseph; therefore, Joseph was always a successful man, even when he was in prison. The Lord accompanied him and granted him grace to endure this trial. Through this, the Lord prepared him for the appointed time.
- He allowed Pharaoh to have dreams that no one could interpret, at a time when the Lord had given Joseph the gift of interpreting dreams. Thus, Joseph interpreted Pharaoh's dreams and entered a new stage of his life as a ruler in Egypt. This was, in fact, an important stage in God's economy for His people Israel, leading towards the fulfilment of the purpose of the coming of the Messiah, the Saviour, who was to come from Israel.

This calls us to pause and reflect in order to understand God's ways in general and to unveil an important matter in His ways and the divine economies.

Understanding God's Ways

There is a special mystery by which the Lord fulfils His purposes:

- God continues to observe humanity patiently—though with pain—yet steadfastly and lovingly. He sees evil increasing, and He knows that evil itself destroys the wicked, as the Psalms say: *'Evil shall slay the wicked'* (Psalm 34:21); *'Let evil hunt the violent man to overthrow him'* (Psalm 140:11). In the end, there is an inevitable judgement, which man brings upon himself and his land as a result of his conduct, for the earth is man's responsibility.

- When the time of judgement draws near, the eyes of the Lord search for the faithful: '*For the eyes of the Lord run to and fro throughout the whole earth, to show Himself strong on behalf of those whose heart is loyal to Him*' (2 Chronicles 16:9).
- While evil increases and judgement draws near, the seed prepared by God becomes ready to be manifested. Through it, God continues to work towards the fulfilment of His plans, and the human race—though it was struck and destroyed by judgement—continues through this seed, whether the judgement is absolute, like the Flood; partial, like that of Sodom and Gomorrah; or local, as might have occurred in Egypt as a result of the famine.
- Therefore, this seed must be found. The prophets called it *the remnant,* as we later read in the books of the prophets. This remnant bears within it a holy seed—God's seed that is preserved within these souls—which continues to be manifested in the descendants until the same tragedy is repeated: the descendants deviate, and evil increases. Then God's work is repeated, as the seed—the remnant that bears within it God's mystery—is found anew.

We must discern the form of judgement occurring in our generation, lest it already be taking place while we are unaware and inattentive.

- It is clear that what determines whether a person bears this mystery—this holy seed—and is prepared to fulfil God's purposes as part of the remnant after judgement is manifested for purification, is the condition of his heart and mind. The heart is the field of God's work. It is also the field of the work of the evil one. If the heart is inclined and directed towards God, the person acquires God's mind—His mindset—which differs from the mindset of one's generation and from life's deadly routine, which is devoid of any true aim that could restore to man his humanity. However, the one who acquires God's mind is restored to himself, restored to God, and restored to the divine purposes. He becomes the *remnant,* whom God has kept and preserved for His will and purposes, and who bears the holy seed referred to in God's promise after the Fall of man: *the seed of the woman who will bruise the head of the serpent*—that is, the awaited Messiah who was to come for salvation.

To conclude this point, let us look at the promises associated with this matter:

> *The secret of the Lord is with those who fear Him, and He will show them His covenant* (Psalm 25:14).

> *Surely the Lord God does nothing, unless He reveals His secret to His servants the prophets* (Amos 3:7).

God does not hide His secrets from those who walk with Him. He reveals them to them clearly, so that they may understand each step of His will.

Our generation is both a generation of judgement and a generation of the remnant. While judgement is being manifested, God is preparing the remnant and revealing His secrets to them.

With this, we conclude the introduction.

The Remnant

After this introductory explanation, we now want to understand the meaning of the word *remnant* as it appears in Scripture. What does this word mean in its biblical context?

The term *remnant* does not merely refer to those who have survived a catastrophe, a destructive war, or the like. Rather, the use of this word in Scripture bears a more specific meaning.

The remnant, in God's mind, consists of those who obey His commandments, maintain a living and renewed fellowship with Him, live in the fear of God, trust in all His promises, and recognise the necessity of undergoing judgement when one chooses to depart from His commandments, reject Him, and become immersed in evil.

When this latter condition prevails, a time comes when the cup of evil becomes full, and judgement is manifested. In such cases, those who practice evil most likely reap the consequences of the life they have lived—whether through catastrophes, death, dispersion, or other forms of destruction.

Amid all this, a faithful remnant is preserved. God keeps and protects them, for through them His will and purposes are fulfilled, and His plan for His people extends from generation to generation and throughout all times and seasons.

The judgement emphasises the inevitability of the consequences of breaking the commandments and breaking the covenant between God and His people, or the consequences of a person breaking his relationship with God and with His commandments.

At this point, the position and role of the remnant become apparent. They, in contrast, emphasise God's mercies and affirm that His plans and purposes can never be cancelled but are fulfilled through those who are faithful. These faithful ones are considered a faithful nucleus with whom the Lord works and through whom He brings about the salvation of humanity and the fulfilment of all things unto the fullness—the consummation of salvation.

We will see that the theme of *the remnant* in Scripture is especially evident in the prophetic books, particularly the Book of Isaiah. However, we also find a clear example of this theme in First Kings 19, in the words of the Lord to Elijah, who came before the Lord lamenting his condition after slaying the prophets of Baal and because of Jezebel's threats.

We read:

> *And behold, the word of the Lord came to him* [to Elijah in Mount Horeb]*, and He said to him, "What are you doing here, Elijah?" So he said, "I have been very zealous for the Lord God of hosts; for the children of Israel have forsaken Your covenant, torn down Your altars, and killed Your prophets with the sword.* ***I alone am left****; and they seek to take my life"* (1 Kings 19:9b, 10).

The Lord replied, saying:

> ***I have reserved seven thousand in Israel,*** *all whose knees have not bowed to Baal, and every mouth that has not kissed him* (1 Kings 19:18).

Here we see a clear picture of the faithful remnant during the time of Elijah (seven thousand). While many—indeed, most—of the people of Israel turned to the worship of Baal, there was a faithful remnant through whom God's will was revealed and fulfilled at that time.

Now, let us follow the theme of the remnant in the prophetic books and see their position and role during difficult times—the times when the people turned away from God and the times of judgement.

The Theme of the Remnant in the Prophetic Books

• Amos the Prophet (8th century BC)

Amos was the first prophet to refer to the remnant—those who were saved from judgement—in the fifth chapter of his prophecy:

> *Seek good and not evil, that you may live; so the Lord God of hosts will be with you, as you have spoken. Hate evil, love good; establish justice in the gate. It may be that the Lord God of hosts will be gracious to* ***the remnant of Joseph*** (Amos 5:14, 15).

• Isaiah the Prophet (740–680 BC)

In this prophecy, we find greater clarity regarding the theme of the remnant. Indeed, what may be called *the theology of the remnant* is especially evident in this book. We will return to study and examine portions of this prophecy because of its importance for us, particularly in the time in which we now live—the end times.

Important points that we need to understand regarding the remnant in the book of Isaiah:

- The connection between judgement, salvation, and holiness
- When judgement is manifested, only a few are preserved and remain—a remnant. Though small, this remnant possesses significant spiritual resources and bears important responsibilities for the future.
- This remnant undergoes purification with fire and becomes holy, bearing a holy seed (Isaiah 6:13; 10:20–22).

> *But yet a tenth will be in it, and will return and be for consuming, as a terebinth tree or as an oak, whose stump remains when it is cut down. So the* ***holy seed*** *shall be its stump* (Isaiah 6:13).

> *And it shall come to pass in that day that* ***the remnant of Israel,*** *and such as have escaped of the house of Jacob, will never again*

> *depend on him who defeated them, but will depend on the Lord, the Holy One of Israel, in truth. The remnant will return,* ***the remnant of Jacob****, to the Mighty God. For though your people, O Israel, be as the sand of the sea,* ***a remnant of them*** *will return; the destruction decreed shall overflow with righteousness* (Isaiah 10:20–22).

Israel had many people who would perish in the judgement, but a remnant was preserved, from whom the Messiah would come.

- This remnant has privileges and responsibilities for the future.

> *It shall come to pass in that day that the Lord shall set His hand again the second time* ***to recover the remnant of His people*** *who are left, from Assyria and Egypt, from Pathros and Cush, from Elam and Shinar, from Hamath and the islands of the sea. He will set up a banner for the nations, and will assemble the outcasts of Israel, and gather together the dispersed of Judah from the four corners of the earth* (Isaiah 11:11, 12).

> *In that day the Lord of hosts will be for a crown of glory and a diadem of beauty* ***to the remnant of His people*** (Isaiah 28:5).

Here we see how the Lord adorns the remnant. First, He purifies them with fire; then, He adorns them, as they will be the ones who reflect Him to others.

> *And the remnant who have escaped of the house of Judah shall again take root downward, and bear fruit upward. For out of Jerusalem shall go* ***a remnant****, and those who escape from Mount Zion. The zeal of the Lord of hosts will do this* (Isaiah 37:31, 32).

In the second half of the Book of Isaiah (chapters 40–66), we find references to the remnant in the end times and to the nations—that is, those who are not Israelites:

> ***Assemble yourselves and come****; draw near together,* ***you survivors of the nations****! ... Turn to me and be saved, all the ends of the earth! For I am God, and there is no other* (Isaiah 45:20a, 22, ESV).

From among these survivors, the Lord sends missionaries to all the nations (universal missionaries):

> *I will set a sign among them; and* ***those among them who escape I will send to the nations****: to Tarshish and Pul and Lud, who draw the bow, and Tubal and Javan, to the coastlands afar off who have not heard My fame nor seen My glory. And they shall declare My glory among the Gentiles* (Isaiah 66:19).

- **Micah the Prophet (7th century BC)**

Micah speaks about the remnant who had been dispersed among the nations. Yet, Yahweh would assemble them and make them a strong nation. Thus, they would be in the midst of the nations like dew (a symbol of life) and like a lion (a symbol of power) until the time of Christ's nativity and the restoration of Israel from her captivity:

> *In that day one shall take up a proverb against you, and lament with a bitter lamentation, saying: 'We are utterly destroyed! He has changed the heritage of my people; how He has removed it from me! To a turncoat He has divided our fields'* (Micah 2:4).

Such was their condition; yet the Lord would gather and assemble the faithful remnant:

> *I will surely assemble all of you, O Jacob, I will surely gather* ***the remnant of Israel****; I will put them together like sheep of the fold, like a flock in the midst of their pasture; they shall make a loud noise because of so many people* (Micah 2:12).

> *I will make the lame* ***a remnant****, and the outcast a strong nation; so the Lord will reign over them in Mount Zion from now on, even forever* (Micah 4:7).

The remnant may be viewed by others as weak, poor, or even in need of help—as though they were broken or lame. However, God's eyes are upon them; He sees their hearts.

The enemy may have caused them to pass through such conditions because he knew that their hearts had been faithful. However, God takes them and makes them into a strong nation, and He reigns over them.

When their appointed time comes, and they have been prepared by God, people will look at them and see life in them at a time when everything else is dry.

Their position in the midst of the nations is like dew and like a lion:

> *Then* ***the remnant*** *of Jacob shall be in the midst of many peoples,* ***like dew*** *from the Lord, like showers on the grass, that tarry for no man nor wait for the sons of men. And* ***the remnant*** *of Jacob shall be among the Gentiles, in the midst of many peoples,* ***like a lion*** *among the beasts of the forest, like a young lion among flocks of sheep, who, if he passes through, both treads down and tears in pieces, and none can deliver* (Micah 5:7, 8).

We find other references to the remnant in the books of the Minor Prophets:

- **Joel**

> *And it shall come to pass that whoever calls on the name of the Lord shall be saved. For in Mount Zion and in Jerusalem there shall be deliverance, as the Lord has said,* ***among the remnant*** *whom the Lord calls* (Joel 2:32).

· Zephaniah

> *I will leave in your midst a meek and humble people, and they shall trust in the name of the Lord.* ***The remnant*** *of Israel shall do no unrighteousness and speak no lies, nor shall a deceitful tongue be found in their mouth; for they shall feed their flocks and lie down, and no one shall make them afraid* (Zephaniah 3:12, 13).

One of the important characteristics of their lives is that they live holy and godly lives, taking heed to their words and judge uprightly[3]. Therefore, they have no fear.

Other references to the remnant in Jeremiah, Ezekiel, and Daniel:

· Jeremiah

> *For thus says the Lord: "Sing with gladness for Jacob, and shout among the chief of the nations; proclaim, give praise, and say, 'O Lord, save Your people,* ***the remnant of Israel****!'"* (Jeremiah 31:7).

Jeremiah was asking God to save the remnant of Israel, for they had been facing great distress as they were about to return from captivity.

· Ezekiel

> *Yet I will leave* ***a remnant,*** *so that you may have some who escape the sword among the nations, when you are scattered through the countries* (Ezekiel 6:8).

Ezekiel was speaking to the people while they were in captivity, telling them that God would preserve a remnant and bring them back.

---

3 John 7:24

Yet behold, there shall be left in it ***a remnant*** *who will be brought out, both sons and daughters; surely they will come out to you, and you will see their ways and their doings. Then you will be comforted concerning the disaster that I have brought upon Jerusalem, all that I have brought upon it* (Ezekiel 14:22).

He was also telling them that they were then reaping the consequences of what they had done; yet the Lord would preserve a remnant and bring them out.

· Daniel

But Daniel purposed in his heart that he ***would not defile himself*** *with the portion of the king's delicacies, nor with the wine which he drank* (Daniel 1:8).

Daniel and his friends (the three youths) are an example of the remnant in their generation.

There were many Israelites in captivity during that time. All of them ate the king's food, justifying themselves by saying that since they were in captivity, they had no choice but to eat it. However, Daniel said, "No, I will obey the commandment, even in captivity."

When everyone does something that breaks the commandment and considers it normal, the remnant say, "No, this is not right." They hold fast to the commandments, even when others abandon the commandments and go astray.

We also read:

But the people who know their God shall be strong, and carry out great exploits (Daniel 11:32b).

The remnant among the nations not only live a godly life, but they also have a role.

A reference to the remnant in the prophetic books after the return from captivity:

• Zechariah

For there shall be a sowing of peace. The vine shall give its fruit, and the ground shall give its produce, and the heavens shall give their dew. And ***I will cause the remnant of this people to possess all these things*** (Zechariah 8:12, ESV).

The Theme of the Remnant in the New Testament

- **Romans 11:** A reference to Israel, and other passages to be discussed later in this study

In this chapter, Apostle Paul refers to the Jews who received faith in Christ as *the remnant.* He speaks about God's plan for Israel and states that there is a remnant who have believed in Christ:

Even so then, at this present time there is ***a remnant*** *according to the election of grace* (Romans 11:5).

What then? Israel has not obtained what it seeks; but the elect have obtained it, and the rest were blinded (Romans 11:7).

Blindness in part has happened to Israel until the fullness of the Gentiles has come in. And so all Israel will be saved (Romans 11:25b, 26a).

We will continue our study of the theme of the remnant by discussing the following four main points:

I. A study of selected passages from the Book of Isaiah
II. Examples of the remnant in the New Testament at the time of Christ's incarnation
III. The connection between curses and their effect on the generations, and the role of the remnant within the economy of redemption
IV. Our responsibility amid this generation, and how we should view the state of the world, the Church, and the remnant

I. A STUDY OF SELECTED PASSAGES FROM THE BOOK OF ISAIAH

A. Isaiah 6

Isaiah had been called to the prophetic ministry and had already completed part of it by this point, as recorded in the first five chapters of his prophecy (Isaiah 1–5).

He had witnessed the condition of the people, who had become greatly estranged from their God; therefore, he directed woes to them. He declared nine woes, as recorded in Isaiah 1:4; 3:9, 11; and 5:8, 11, 18, 20, 21, 22.

Then King Uzziah, who had supported the prophet in his ministry, died. Amid such circumstances—the spiritual state of the people and the death of the king—the prophet seemed to have entered into confusion and pain. He knew that he needed to pour himself out before the Lord, complaining about the condition of the people and seeking rest, comfort, and guidance regarding what he should do.

Yet something unexpected happened: The Lord appeared to the prophet. Thus, instead of complaining about the people to whom he had declared the woes, he cried out concerning himself, saying: '*Woe is me, for I am undone!*' (Isaiah 6:5).

Let us read this passage in chapter 6 of his prophecy:

> *In the year that King Uzziah died, I saw the Lord sitting on a throne, high and lifted up, and the train of His robe filled the temple. Above it stood seraphim; each one had six wings: with two he covered his face, with two he covered his feet, and with two he flew. And one cried to another and said: "Holy, holy, holy is the Lord of hosts; the whole earth is full of His glory!" And the posts*

of the door were shaken by the voice of him who cried out, and the house was filled with smoke. So I said: "Woe is me, for I am undone! Because I am a man of unclean lips, and I dwell in the midst of a people of unclean lips; for my eyes have seen the King, the Lord of hosts." Then one of the seraphim flew to me, having in his hand a live coal which he had taken with the tongs from the altar. And he touched my mouth with it, and said: "Behold, this has touched your lips; your iniquity is taken away, and your sin purged" (Isaiah 6:1–7).

At this point, in the presence of God, the prophet realised that the problem was not only with the people, but that he himself also needed deep cleansing so that he might perceive God's purposes and know how to deal with the people in their present condition.

Seeing his own sin, the prophet cried out, seeking purification. Because his cry was sincere, he received an immediate response. One of the seraphim flew to him with a purifying coal from the heavenly altar, purified him, and declared to him his new state: *'Your iniquity is taken away, and your sin is purged'* (Isaiah 6:7).

At this point, he heard the voice of the Lord calling him once again to a new mission—for he had already been sent as a prophet and had served the people during the previous stage, but he had paused because he did not know what to do with the people in their current state. Now, after recognising his need for purification and receiving it, he heard the Lord's voice calling him anew. Let us read:

Also I heard the voice of the Lord, saying: "Whom shall I send, and who will go for Us?" Then I said, "Here am I! Send me" (Isaiah 6:8).

Although the prophet knew that he had already been sent to serve the people, he realised that he needed renewal of his sending forth.

Therefore, as soon as he heard the Lord asking who would go, he replied: *"Here am I! Send me."*

What was this new mission?

The prophet might have thought:

What could he possibly say to the people after having declared all these woes to them, and was there any possibility that they would take heed and repent?

At this point, the word of the Lord came to him concerning his new mission and what he was to say to this stubborn people. Let us read:

> *And He said, "Go, and tell this people: 'Keep on hearing, but do not understand; keep on seeing, but do not perceive.' Make the heart of this people dull, and their ears heavy, and shut their eyes; lest they see with their eyes, and hear with their ears, and understand with their heart, and return and be healed"* (Isaiah 6:9, 10).

These were clear words of judgement that the Lord was now proclaiming against this people. This means that they had exhausted their opportunities to repent. This is a matter that we ought to comprehend and be aware of: When a person exhausts every opportunity for repentance and still does not repent, judgement comes! The prophet himself might have been astonished; perhaps he expected that the Lord would give him a new message (new words) for the people. However, since judgement had already been declared by the Lord, the prophet, in his astonishment, then said the following to the Lord. Let us read:

> *Then I said, "Lord, how long?" And He answered: "Until the cities are laid waste and without inhabitant, the houses are without a man, the land is utterly desolate, the Lord has removed men far away, and the forsaken places are many in the midst of the land"* (Isaiah 6:11, 12).

The prophet asked in astonishment, "How long will the judgement last?" The Lord answered him, and from the Lord's reply the prophet understood that the judgement would be long and severe: the houses would be destroyed, the land would become desolate, and the people would die or be sent far away from their land. All this indeed came to pass when Israel was taken into captivity for seventy years in a distant land. This occurred after the enemy came—first Assyria, and then Babylon—killing, destroying, and laying everything waste.

What a dreadful judgement that came as a result of the people's continual stubbornness, despite God's continual calls to them!

Even more astonishing is what the Lord continued to say to the prophet in the final verse of this chapter, verse 13:

> *But yet a tenth will be in it, and will return and be for consuming, as a terebinth tree or as an oak, whose stump remains when it is cut down. So the holy seed shall be its stump* (Isaiah 6:13).

Despite the vast destruction—so severe that most of the people would either die or be taken captive, leaving only one tenth—this remaining tenth would also stand under the sentence of judgement. Perhaps God had seen in them some willingness to respond and therefore gave them another opportunity. Yet, sadly, they did not take heed because of their hardened hearts, and so they too came under judgement. Thus, even this tenth would be consumed.

What then would become of this nation? Would Israel be utterly wiped out? Would their land cease to exist? No—for who could overturn the Lord's faithful promises, even when these promises had been given to a treacherous, rebellious, and stubborn people?!

The Lord has another mystery: He has a hidden seed, hidden in the ground, like a tree that has been cut down and a small stump remains. It is small and hardly visible, yet that hidden stump remains beneath the soil, bearing the life of the tree. Thus, it begins to grow again and extend upwards. But now it grows in a healthier and renewed state, unlike its former condition. This is exactly what happened with Israel—with those whom the prophets called *the faithful remnant.*

They were but a handful of people (a small group of people), scarcely noticed by anyone. Yet, amid the wars, the destruction, and the captivity, the eyes of the Lord were upon them, for they obeyed Him, lived in the fear of God, and kept His commandments. The Lord loved them, and He knew that through them He would fulfil His purposes after the process of deep purification would be completed. This was the remnant mentioned at the beginning of this book of Scripture. We will follow God's economy concerning this remnant, so that we may gain understanding and attentiveness to perceive what the Lord desires to say to us through this study about the remnant and its economy as revealed in the Scriptures.

Note:

- Remember that we are not studying the book of Isaiah, but rather the theme of the remnant. Nevertheless, we must say that this book of Scripture presents the theme of the remnant in the clearest way—particularly with regard to its economy, God's promises to it, and His purposes for it, as we shall see.
- There are various references to this theme throughout this book of Scripture. However, it would be difficult to examine them all, for in doing so we might lose the focus needed to connect the truths related to the economy of the remnant so as to gain understanding and discern the divine purpose required of us.

What happened after the events recorded in Chapter 6?

The prophet attempted to help King Ahaz, who had backslidden in his faith, by delivering to him a message from the Lord (Isaiah 7). However, the king did not respond. Consequently, the manifestations of judgement began to unfold quickly. The powerful enemy that was about to invade, destroy, and carry the people into captivity soon appeared—Assyria and its armies (Isaiah 8).

At this point, the prophet immediately understood the significance of the economy that the Lord had told him about—the stump bearing a holy seed. Therefore, he decided to go into seclusion. He left the ministry to the people in order to focus on the small handful—the remnant—who were to be prepared to fulfil God's purposes. This remnant, this small group, were his disciples. Let us now read what the Lord said to him at that time:

> *Bind up the testimony, seal the law among my disciples. And I will wait on the Lord, who hides His face from the house of Jacob; and I will hope in Him. Here am I and the children whom the Lord has given me! We are for signs and wonders in Israel from the Lord of hosts, who dwells in Mount Zion* (Isaiah 8:16–18).

God told Isaiah to leave ministering to the people and focus on his disciples. The prophet responded to the Lord and did exactly that.

There was destruction and desolation everywhere, yet the Lord described this remnant—this small group—as *'signs and wonders in Israel'*. This indicates that God was carrying out two activities simultaneously:

- One activity was to increase the judgement, because the people were unresponsive and their unresponsiveness continued to increase.
- The other activity was to purify and adorn the remnant.

The prophet withdrew and entered a time of seclusion with his disciples in order to be prepared, and the Lord helped him understand the following:

- The Lord would hide His face from Israel; this meant that judgement was being manifested. In Isaiah 45:15, the prophet says, *'Truly You are God, who hide Yourself, O God of Israel'*.
- There would be a time of waiting to prepare the remnant. This is often part of God's salvific economy to prepare the persons who need to be made ready for what is to come.
- The prophet had to go into seclusion with his disciples to complete this preparation. The Lord revealed to him that those disciples were a distinguished, chosen group. They were signs and wonders because they would be the remnant who would inherit all God's promises and fulfil all His plans!

Although the prophet had then entered into a spiritual retreat and a time of preparation with his disciples, he declared woes against the people. However, he no longer declared them as he had at first, in order to awaken the people for them to repent (for that time or opportunity had ended). Instead, he now declared them as a manifestation of judgement:

> *Woe to those who decree unrighteous decrees ...* (Isaiah 10:1).

The prophet also declared woes against the nation that was coming to ruin and destroy them—Assyria. This is because Assyria was but a tool used by God to fulfil His purpose in chastening and purifying His people and land; yet they (the Assyrians) considered themselves as having absolute power and authority, as though God were absent from the scene:

> *Woe to Assyria, the rod of My anger and the staff in whose hand is My indignation* (Isaiah 10:5).

Amid all this, we once again hear the prophet refer to the remnant that was being prepared in the midst of this destruction:

> *And it shall come to pass in that day that* ***the remnant of Israel,*** *and such as have escaped of the house of Jacob, will never again depend on him who defeated them, but will depend on the Lord, the Holy One of Israel, in truth.* ***The remnant will return, the remnant of Jacob, to the Mighty God*** (Isaiah 10:20, 21).

What happened after that? How and when was this remnant manifested in order to fulfil its work in God's economy?

There is something else that must be manifested so that the remnant may be qualified and released into the work. The prophet referred to this matter implicitly in chapter 11, but at the appropriate time he would reveal it fully and explicitly; we will then see and understand the work that this remnant was to carry out.

What is the matter referred to in chapter 11?

Let us read:

> *There shall come forth a Rod from the stem of Jesse, and a Branch shall grow out of his roots. The Spirit of the Lord shall rest upon Him, the Spirit of wisdom and understanding, the Spirit of counsel and might, the Spirit of knowledge and of the fear of the Lord* (Isaiah 11:1, 2).

Why does the prophet then proclaim this following passage here, presenting a very strange and unfamiliar picture:

> *The wolf also shall dwell with the lamb, the leopard shall lie down with the young goat, the calf and the young lion and the fatling together; and a little child shall lead them. The cow and the bear shall graze; their young ones shall lie down together; and the lion shall eat straw like the ox. The nursing child shall play by the*

> *cobra's hole, and the weaned child shall put his hand in the viper's den. They shall not hurt nor destroy in all My holy mountain, for the earth shall be full of the knowledge of the Lord as the waters cover the sea. And in that day there shall be a Root of Jesse, who shall stand as a banner to the people; for the Gentiles shall seek Him, and His resting place shall be glorious* (Isaiah 11:6–10).

What is this revelation about?

It is about the Messiah who was to come for salvation.

The truth of the matter is that the full fulfilment of all that is mentioned here will take place at the second coming of Christ to reign. However, this revelation about the Messiah is mentioned here because the messiah calling must work with the remnant to fulfil all God's purposes.

We will later see and understand more about the connection between the manifestation of the messiah calling and the manifestation of the remnant. Throughout divine history, in all generations, these two manifestations worked together in accomplishing God's purposes—after the evil one would have deceived humans and distanced them from God. As the generations pass, a break occurs in the divine economy. In order to restore that economy once more, the messiah (that is, the messiah calling) and the remnant (the faithful who are preserved amid difficult circumstances and times of judgement) must be manifested, so that they may work together and God's purposes may continue towards their appointed goal: the coming of Christ. This happened at His first coming (His incarnation), and it will also be true at His second coming (His reign)!

Now, let us go directly to speaking about the messiah calling—although from time to time, the prophet refers to the remnant in various chapters, as we read in the introduction.

B. Isaiah 53

These prophetic words have two dimensions:

- The Messiah Himself (Christ)
- The 'messiah calling' or the 'messianic calling'[4]

> *Who has believed our report? And to whom has the arm of the Lord been revealed? For He shall grow up before Him as a tender plant, and as a root out of dry ground. He has no form or comeliness; and when we see Him, there is no beauty that we should desire Him. He is despised and rejected by men, a Man of sorrows and acquainted with grief. And we hid, as it were, our faces from Him; He was despised, and we did not esteem Him. Surely He has borne our griefs and carried our sorrows; yet we esteemed Him stricken, smitten by God, and afflicted. But He was wounded for our transgressions, He was bruised for our iniquities; the chastisement for our peace was upon Him, and by His stripes we are healed* (Isaiah 53:1–5).

He then continues:

> *Yet it pleased the Lord to bruise Him; He has put Him to grief. When You make His soul an offering for sin, He shall see His seed, He shall prolong His days, and the pleasure of the Lord shall prosper in His hand. He shall see the labour of His soul, and be satisfied. By His knowledge My righteous Servant shall justify many, for He shall bear their iniquities* (Isaiah 53:10, 11).

1. These prophetic words which we have just read apply in their full meaning to Jesus Christ, who endured suffering and shame—even unto death on the cross—but rose again,

---

4 The terms 'messiah calling' or 'messianic calling, as used in this book, refer to individuals called to be messiahs in their generation, bearing the features of the Suffering Christ and in whom Christ is formed. Together with the remnant, they have a specific role in the end times, which we will explain in detail throughout this study.

conquering death and annulling every evil economy designed to put souls to death and slay the visions—the visions of faith and the visions of the Kingdom of God!

2. Yet these words are also partially fulfilled in those who are called to the messiah calling, as they enter into this calling through a mystery! It is not granted to them or made manifest until they are first tested, so that it may be revealed how closely they conform to the image of the Messiah. They may possess fragmented spiritual longings that have not yet been purified or seasoned with salt and with fire—the fire of the Holy Spirit:

> *For everyone* ***will be seasoned with fire,*** *and every sacrifice* ***will be seasoned with salt****. Salt is good, but if the salt loses its flavour, how will you season it? Have salt in yourselves, and have peace with one another* (Mark 9:49, 50).

Thus, the Holy Spirit continues to test the person in order to purify him from his own thoughts and to reveal other matters in his life that require purification. He continues this work until He sees the steadfastness and faithfulness of the person towards God's Kingdom and the things of God—a steadfastness that endures regardless of God's gifts or what He permits, whether comfort or suffering!

Both the remnant and those who have a messianic calling require deep purification with fire, for if either of these two callings is not deeply purified and the ego crucified, the divine economy will be marred. Those who are called to the messiah calling receive God's will and then reveal it to the remnant. However, the ego can distort their reception of it. It can become mixed—a mixture of spirit, mind, and soul. Likewise, if the ego of the remnant is not crucified, conflicts driven by the fallen soul may arise among them, as each seeks status or a distinct role. This, in turn, causes them to fall outside of God's true purpose/use for them as His instruments and thus lose their calling as the remnant.

After this inner work of testing and purification, the Lord anoints this person with the messiah calling. In other words, the Spirit of God begins to lead him in the footsteps of Christ while at the same time forming Christ within him—the Christ of suffering and of the path of Golgotha—in order to enter him into the mystery of resurrection deposited in the messiah calling. It is a path of thorns, suffering, and tears; yet it is also a path of supreme divine consolation. It is a path of fellowship in Christ's death, and, at the same time, a path of fellowship in Christ's resurrection. It is a prolonged path of shame and reproach, yet it is also a path of partaking in the glory in Christ Jesus!

3. This path and calling bear within them mysteries of many dimensions. Among these mysteries is the saying we read in verse 11:

By His knowledge My righteous ***Servant*** *shall justify many, for He shall bear their iniquities* (Isaiah 53:11).

These words fully apply to Christ, for He is called *'the Servant'* in Scripture, especially in the book of Isaiah. Therefore, by knowing Christ as Lord, Saviour, and God, a person is justified, because Christ bears his iniquities.

How, then, is this to be understood in relation to the messiah calling? Who can justify others? Christ alone can justify! Yet here lies a mystery known as *redemptive suffering.* This is what we now need to understand through God's grace and the work of His Spirit in us:

Christ alone bears iniquities and justifies the unrighteous. Therefore, receiving this calling means that Christ must first be formed within the person, in the image of the Suffering Christ—the

Christ of Golgotha. When the main/central part of this formation is complete, the Spirit of God begins to reveal the mystery to the one called to bear it—the one called to the Messiah's calling. He reveals to him why his journey has been and still will be filled with suffering, thorns and thistles, closed doors, long waiting, reproach, being misunderstood by others, and so on.

4. The Spirit of God reveals to the person that the Christ being formed within him is the Christ who bears iniquities and justifies the unrighteous. Therefore, some of the iniquities of others are laid upon him.

This may prompt the question: What is this person's fault?

In fact, the iniquities laid upon him are ones in which he himself participates. This means he himself has iniquities of his own, and the Lord deals with them through the mystery of redemption. However, since he is called to be a messiah—a small Christ—the Holy Spirit also lays upon him the iniquities of others that are of the same kind as his own. Thus, he would be carrying his own iniquities and the iniquities of others.

Yet because the Spirit of God works in him through the mystery of Christ's redemption, a time will come when his diligence and suffering are complete, and his iniquities will fall away. Consequently, the iniquities of others that have been laid upon him will fall away as well. He will then hear the voice:

> *"Comfort, yes, comfort My people!" says your God. "Speak comfort to Jerusalem* [to the man of God who is called to the Messiah's calling], *and cry out to her, that her warfare is ended, that her iniquity is pardoned* [both her own iniquity and the iniquity of others which she bore: *'He shall bear their iniquities'*]; *for she has received from the Lord's hand double for all her sins"* (Isaiah 40:1, 2).

5. Why is it 'double' when God is fair and righteous?

This is because her own iniquities, together with the iniquities laid upon her, require a double portion: one part for herself and the other for those whose iniquities were laid upon her. Thus, justification is granted to both: *'By His knowledge ... shall justify many'*!

6. After understanding all this, the person's heart rests completely in God's matters; it rests in Christ the Messiah, and becomes united with Him. Looking back at the past, the person understands why he had to endure all the contempt: *'He is despised and rejected by men, a Man of sorrows and acquainted with grief'* (Isaiah 53:3). He understands why his image had been marred, even though he always sought not to cause anyone to stumble by his conduct. Now, he understands that this is part of his messianic calling, for it is written of Him: *'He has no form or comeliness; and when we see Him, there is no beauty that we should desire Him'* (Isaiah 53:2).

He will also understand why he had always been accused of surely having committed many mistakes and grave sins, making his path filled with thorns and closed doors. However, he now comes to understand the words of Scripture that say: *'Surely He has borne our griefs and carried our sorrows; yet we esteemed Him stricken, smitten by God, and afflicted'* (Isaiah 53:4).

In this way, the mysteries of the messiah calling are revealed. Through unity with the true Messiah, to whom alone belong these words in their fullness, anyone called to the messiah calling can carry out and complete his calling as a messiah in its partial form, yet he receives the fullness of the work of redemption that Christ—the Messiah for all—has completed.

Now, let us speak about the remnant.

C. Isaiah 54:1–3; 58:12; 61:1–4

Isaiah 54:1–3

"Sing, O barren, you who have not borne! Break forth into singing, and cry aloud, you who have not laboured with child! For more are the children of the desolate than the children of the married woman," says the Lord. "Enlarge the place of your tent, and let them stretch out the curtains of your dwellings; do not spare; lengthen your cords, and strengthen your stakes. For you shall expand to the right and to the left, and your descendants will inherit the nations, and make the desolate cities inhabited."

Isaiah 58:12

Those from among you shall build the old waste places; you shall raise up the foundations of many generations; and you shall be called the Repairer of the Breach, the Restorer of Streets to Dwell In.

Isaiah 61:1–4

"The Spirit of the Lord God is upon Me, because the Lord has anointed Me to preach good tidings to the poor; He has sent Me to heal the brokenhearted, to proclaim liberty to the captives, and the opening of the prison to those who are bound; to proclaim the acceptable year of the Lord, and the day of vengeance of our God; to comfort all who mourn, to console those who mourn in Zion, to give them beauty for ashes, the oil of joy for mourning, the garment of praise for the spirit of heaviness; that they may be called trees of righteousness, the planting of the Lord, that He may be glorified." And they shall rebuild the old ruins, they shall raise up the former desolations, and they shall repair the ruined cities, the desolations of many generations.

In these biblical passages, we notice the following:

There is desolation, yet there is also a need to rebuild:

> *Your descendants will inherit the nations, and make the desolate cities inhabited* (Isaiah 54:3).
>
> *Shall build the old waste places* (Isaiah 58:12).
>
> *And they shall rebuild the old ruins ... and they shall repair the ruined cities* (Isaiah 61:4).

What does this mean?

1. A judgement must have taken place, resulting in this destruction—whether through wars that came upon Israel because of their disobedience to God, or through the absence of blessing, the lack of rain, and poor harvests. As a result, the land became desolate.
2. Yet there is a call to rebuild. To whom is this divine call directed? It is directed to the faithful remnant. In the midst of this destruction, God preserved a small group; they were rescued from the wars, dangers, and ruin.
3. This small group was not merely lucky to have survived. Rather, they were preserved according to a divine economy. God protected them because of their obedience and faithfulness.
4. Here lies an important matter we ought to understand: this divine protection was not merely the preservation of their lives from death or destruction, but the preservation of *the holy seed* found within them, as we read in Isaiah 6:13.
5. From this holy seed, all would be rebuilt. Therefore, the Lord called upon them to rebuild. This means that they were given a missionary work. They were now on a mission; they were sent by the Lord to arise and build the waste places.

6. Moreover, the hand of the Lord would work with them. Therefore, they would expand ('*Lengthen your cords ... For you shall expand to the right and to the left*') and they would even inherit nations for the sake of the Kingdom of God.
7. There is another remarkable matter that we need to pay attention to, mentioned in Isaiah 61:1–4. It is evident that this remnant endured many kinds of suffering. They are those referred to in this passage as '*the captives*', '*those who are bound*', and '*those who mourn in Zion*'. They experienced *sorrow, mourning,* and *a spirit of heaviness.* They even became *ashes,* and *all their beauty was gone.* They resembled their Saviour, of whom it is written: '*He has no form or comeliness; and when we see Him, there is no beauty that we should desire Him*' (Isaiah 53:2).
8. Here we see the connection between the Messiah and the remnant. The Messiah was anointed to begin His work. It is clear that His main work was among those whom He knew well. Thus, He proclaimed liberty to the captives and the opening of the prison to those who were bound; He comforted those who mourned, and gave them beauty for ashes and the garment of praise for the spirit of heaviness.[5] Through this, they were prepared for mission, and then He sent them forth to rebuild the old waste places and repair the ruined cities.

A closer examination of these passages (Isaiah 58 and Isaiah 54):

Isaiah 58

> ***Those from among you*** *shall build the* ***old waste places; You shall raise up the foundations of many generations;*** *and*

5 Isaiah 61:1–3

> ***you shall be called the Repairer of the Breach,*** *the Restorer of Streets to Dwell In* (Isaiah 58:12).

- *Those from among you*

This does not refer to a biological descendant, but to a spiritual descendant who lives in righteousness and walks according to the Spirit. Unlike the biological descendant, this spiritual descendant does not focus only on the outward form of fasting described in Isaiah 58, which God rejected, as it consists merely of external practices while the person's life remains far from God's commandments:

> *Indeed you fast for strife and debate, and to strike with the fist of wickedness. You will not fast as you do this day, to make your voice heard on high. Is it a fast that I have chosen ...* (Isaiah 58:4, 5a).

(*'... to make your voice heard on high ...'* This phrase means that God wants to hear our voices of prayer. When we fast, it is as though we put a microphone to our lips and pray!)

Thus, they are not a biological descendant, but a spiritual one. They have a spiritual identity; therefore, they can be entrusted with the spiritual rebuilding, through which the societies in all their human sectors are also built.

- *Old waste places*

The reference here is not to the cities destroyed during the captivity, but to the general state of collapse in Israel—economically, educationally, and morally.

Through this remnant and the rebuilding they were to undertake, the society would change. They would rebuild society in all its fields and sectors.

When economic collapse occurs within a society, it affects morality and education. This, in fact, reflects a picture of judgement.

Think of the country in which you live: if this picture is present, it may indicate judgement. We must discern the judgement from its very beginning. When we see economic collapse, it may not simply be a temporary crisis, but a manifestation of judgement.

- *You shall raise up the foundations of many generations*

This refers to the continuity of the new state. It is achieved by perceiving God's covenants with His people and renewing the covenants from generation to generation without interruption. This is an important sign or characteristic of the remnant: They deal with the history in which the relationship with God was broken and interrupted, as we see in Israel's history during the time of the kings recorded in the Books of Kings and Chronicles.

- *You shall be called the Repairer of the Breach*

This presents Israel in a new picture, after addressing breaches. It also involves a continuous missionary work that proclaims the God of Israel.

Isaiah 54

> *Enlarge the place of your tent ... Lengthen your cords ...* ***For you shall expand to the right and to the left****, and* ***your descendants will inherit the nations****, and* ***make the desolate cities inhabited*** (Isaiah 54:2, 3).

Not only is there a rebuilding of the waste places and a repairing of the breaches, but there is also expansion, blessing, enlargement, and prosperity:

> *Behold, I will lay your stones with colourful gems, and lay your foundations with sapphires. I will make your pinnacles of rubies,*

your gates of crystal, and all your walls of precious stones. All your children shall be taught by the Lord, and great shall be the peace of your children (Isaiah 54:11–13).

- *Your descendants will inherit the nations*

This signifies that the redemption of the nations will occur when Israel is restored. In Isaiah 49–55, the section that refers to the Lord's Servant—the Messiah—we see the nations returning to Zion (For example, Isaiah 49:18–21). In the same chapter, we read:

I will also give You as a light to the Gentiles, that You should be My salvation to the ends of the earth (Isaiah 49:6b).

This is the calling of the messiah: it expands, and it bears light and salvation.

- *Make the desolate cities inhabited*

This does not refer merely to the physical reconstruction of ruined cities, but rather to spiritual rebuilding through restoration to the covenant with God and comprehensive renewal.

- *For you shall expand to the right and to the left*

Who will bring about this expansion?

The Lord Jesus will; He is the one who will establish Zion:

But you have come to Mount Zion and to the city of the living God, the heavenly Jerusalem, to an innumerable company of angels, to the general assembly and church of the firstborn who are registered in heaven, to God the Judge of all, to the spirits of just men made perfect, to Jesus the Mediator of the new covenant, and to the blood of sprinkling that speaks better things than that of Abel (Hebrews 12:22–24).

He is also the one who declared the global mission:

You shall be witnesses to Me in Jerusalem, and in all Judea and Samaria, and to the end of the earth (Acts 1:8).

Application:

The first level is to apply this personally:

- To rebuild the desolate areas in our souls caused by wounds, bondages, or ruins that have occurred over the years
- To build a steadfast relationship with God through regular, continual prayer and reading the Word of God
- To build a conscience cleansed by the blood of Jesus and washed from any sense of guilt or shame

In the Spirit, all these are considered desolate places and ruined areas.

Second: To cooperate together for the restoration of the desolate spiritual communities (the church is a spiritual community):

- To build spiritual practices—not merely external forms such as the rejected fast described in Isaiah 58
- To build healthy spiritual relationships

Third: To participate in the missionary work, according to the leading of the Holy Spirit, in places, countries, and communities that wait for sound spiritual rebuilding.

In summary, there are three levels of application:

- The personal level
- The corporate level of the church (the community of believers)
- The missionary dimension under the leading of the Holy Spirit

Warnings:

- Avoid an arrogant or haughty attitude towards others or towards the desolate places.
- Avoid times of despair and frustration because of the widespread ruin around us.
- Avoid neglecting our responsibility and mission.

II. EXAMPLES OF THE REMNANT IN THE NEW TESTAMENT AT THE TIME OF CHRIST'S INCARNATION

Here are some clear examples that represent the remnant at the time of Christ's incarnation:

Zacharias and Elizabeth

First, we must recall the words of Christ concerning the generation living at the time of His incarnation and the way He described it.

He said about it:[6]

> *An evil and adulterous generation* (Matthew 12:39).
> *This adulterous and sinful generation* (Mark 8:38).
> *O faithless generation* (Mark 9:19).
> *O faithless and twisted generation* (Luke 9:41, ESV).

Shortly afterward, during his ministry, Apostle Paul wrote to the church in Philippi, describing that generation as: *'a crooked and perverse generation'* (Philippians 2:15).

Such was the condition of Israel. They were meant to present a correct picture and serve as a model to the world; yet this was their state. This indicates that they were under judgement. The words of Jesus to the scribes and Pharisees further confirm that a state of judgement had come upon them.

Where was the remnant in the midst of judgement, which had only just begun?[7]

---

6 See also Matthew 12:45; 16:4; 17:17; Luke 11:29.

7 Later, in AD 70—about thirty-five years after the ascension of Christ—Titus, the Roman general, destroyed Jerusalem. This was a full manifestation of judgement.

In the midst of this generation, there was a couple whom the Bible describes as follows:

> *And they were both righteous before God, walking in all the commandments and ordinances of the Lord blameless* (Luke 1:6).

These were Zacharias and Elizabeth. They represent a true picture of the faithful remnant—obedient to the Lord and blameless.

Thus, God found whom He had been seeking: *the righteous who were walking in all the commandments and ordinances of the Lord blameless.*

Why was God searching for such righteous people?

Because He had a specific request, or rather an important need for His people, Israel.

What was this need?

God wanted a prophetic voice through whom He could speak to the people.

The prophetic voice had ceased for 400 years. Therefore, God was seeking vessels through which He could once again speak prophetically to His people, as He had done in former times. As it is written in Hebrews 1:1:

> *God, who at various times and in various ways spoke in time past to the fathers by the prophets.*

Finally, the Lord found whom He had been seeking. He found the faithful remnant. He found Zacharias and Elizabeth.

Now what would God do? He would begin to prepare them for what He wanted. In accordance with the divine economy, it was time for the prophet who had been foretold of in the prophetic books to appear, as we read in Isaiah and Malachi:

> *The voice of one crying in the wilderness: "Prepare the way of the Lord; make straight in the desert a highway for our God"* (Isaiah 40:3).

Later on, John the Baptist himself referred to this when he was asked about his identity, as recorded in the Gospel of John:

> *Then they said to him, "Who are you, that we may give an answer to those who sent us? What do you say about yourself?" He said: "I am 'The voice of one crying in the wilderness: "Make straight the way of the Lord,"' as the prophet Isaiah said* (John 1:22, 23).

The prophet Malachi also wrote about him:

> *"Behold, I send My messenger, and he will prepare the way before Me. And the Lord, whom you seek, will suddenly come to His temple, even the Messenger of the covenant, in whom you delight. Behold, He is coming," Says the Lord of hosts* (Malachi 3:1).

Therefore, the prophetic vessel whom the Lord was seeking was not merely like the other prophets, but a very special one; for he would come before the Messiah to prepare the way for Him. The angel who announced the birth of John the Baptist to Zacharias testified to this:

> *But the angel said to him, "Do not be afraid, Zacharias, for your prayer is heard; and your wife Elizabeth will bear you a son, and you shall call his name John. And you will have joy and gladness, and many will rejoice at his birth. For* ***he will be great in the sight of the Lord****, and shall drink neither wine nor strong drink. He will also be filled with the Holy Spirit, even from his mother's womb. And he will turn many of the children of Israel to the Lord their God. He will also go before Him in the spirit and power of Elijah, 'to turn the hearts of the fathers to the children,' and the disobedient to the wisdom of the just, to make ready a people prepared for the Lord"* (Luke 1:13–17).

Jesus Himself testified of him:

> *As they* [the two disciples of the Baptist who were sent by him to the Lord Jesus] *departed, Jesus began to say to the multitudes concerning John: "What did you go out into the wilderness to see? A reed shaken by the wind? But what did you go out to see? A man clothed in soft garments? Indeed, those who wear soft clothing are in kings' houses. But what did you go out to see? A prophet? Yes, I say to you, and more than a prophet. For this is he of whom it is written: 'Behold,* ***I send My messenger before Your face, who will prepare Your way before You.****' Assuredly, I say to you,* ***among those born of women there has not risen one greater than John the Baptist****; but he who is least in the kingdom of heaven is greater than he"* (Matthew 11:7–11).

In another passage, recorded in the Gospel of John, the Lord Jesus also testified about him before the Jews, saying:

> *He was the burning and shining lamp, and you were willing for a time to rejoice in his light* (John 5:35).

From these testimonies—the angel's and the Lord Jesus'—we understand the character and responsibilities of the prophetic vessel whom the Lord was seeking at that time.

Therefore, after finding Zacharias and Elizabeth, the Lord began to prepare them. But how did this preparation take place?

The Lord prepared them through purification by fire, as we see, for example, in how He purified the prophet Isaiah with a burning coal taken from the heavenly altar (Isaiah 6).

Practically, this purification by fire took place through their prolonged barrenness. For the Jews, according to the Law, this condition was considered a source of shame or reproach, and, moreover, it signified the presence of hidden sin or something displeasing to God in their life.

How painful this must have been for them, especially since Zacharias was a priest and would normally be seen as blessed by God. To be barren, then, must have been very painful. How deeply broken they were by the disapproving eyes and the comments of others, which continued and extended over many years, even into their old age!

It had thus become clear that God had not yet answered their prayers. How often they had prayed and asked of the Lord, as evident in the words of the angel when he went to Zacharias to announce the birth of John the Baptist. How painful it must have been for the priest who encouraged others to pray, assuring them that God would answer, yet was himself seen as having prayed but whose prayers seemed rejected because he had not received a response!

However, all of this was part of God's plan for their preparation.

Another element in God's plan for their preparation was leaving them barren until they had passed childbearing age. This is what Zacharias said to the angel who came to him with the announcement:

> *And Zacharias said to the angel, "How shall I know this? For I am an old man, and my wife is well advanced in years"* (Luke 1:18).

However, God had a specific purpose in this. He desired a holy descendant who was not conceived according to lust, but through a special divine intervention. In this way, this descendant would be entirely pure and free from any lust.

In the end, John the Baptist was precisely the person God wanted him to be. He was described as the angel who came before the Lord, signifying his angelic nature.

Can you see what the remnant can accomplish? They can change the course of history!

The Baptist came as a voice calling for repentance in a generation dominated by the scribes and Pharisees—yet no one could stop him. As soon as he began his ministry, all went out to him and were baptised (Matthew 3:5, 6; Luke 3:3).

In Matthew 3:7, we read how he rebuked the Pharisees and Sadducees, who held religious authority, saying to them: *'Brood of vipers! Who warned you to flee from the wrath to come?'* He was a prophet strengthened with divine power and used mightily by God. He was a prophet with specific characteristics in order to prepare the way for the coming of the Messiah.

Let us now consider some divine highlights in this unique event—the birth of the prophet sent to prepare the way for the divine incarnation:

- ***With Zacharias***

But the angel said to him, "Do not be afraid, Zacharias, for ***your prayer is heard****; and your wife Elizabeth will bear you a son, and you shall call his name John"* (Luke 1:13).

The angel tells Zacharias that God had heard his prayers: "You, Zacharias, may think that your prayers were not heard, but they have indeed been heard!"

The name Zacharias means 'God remembers'. In ancient times, the names given to the people of Israel carried special significance. God intended for him to be called Zacharias because one day he would learn that God never forgets any prayer offered before Him, for He always remembers.

Is this not a lesson that we all need to learn as well—especially if we understand our responsibility as the remnant and how the remnant are prepared? The lesson is this: God remembers, and He never forgets!

Here we need to recall that Zacharias had an example who came before him. As a priest, he must have known and studied the holy history well; therefore, he would have been familiar with what happened with Abraham and Sarah. Why, then, did he doubt when the angel announced that he would have a son?

Because of this doubt, a temporary judgement was laid upon him, and he was to remain mute until the fulfilment of the matter he had doubted. The angel said to him:

> *But behold, you will be mute and not able to speak until the day these things take place, because you did not believe my words which will be fulfilled in their own time* (Luke 1:20).

Does this not draw our attention to the fact that God wants us to believe Him—even in wondrous matters—because this reveals Him as a wondrous God, who works wonders:

> *Who is like You, O Lord, among the gods? Who is like You, glorious in holiness, fearful in praises, doing wonders?* (Exodus 15:11).

We also notice that the angel told Zacharias the name of his son who was to be born: *'You shall call his name John'*. The name John means 'God is compassionate'. Can we see how God desires not only that we trust Him, but also that we know His attributes—that He is a compassionate God?

God desires that the remnant truly know Him—know His attributes and His character—because they are called to proclaim Him to others. The remnant must understand that God is faithful: He hears prayers and answers them, yet He does so according to His perfect timing. The difficulty that causes us to stumble or take offense is that we often desire a timing different from His.

Let us look at some excerpts of Zacharias' prophecy, which he proclaimed when John was born and his mouth was opened and his tongue loosed, and he praised God (Luke 1:64).

> *The Lord God of Israel … has visited and redeemed His people* (Luke 1:68).

'To perform the mercy promised to our fathers and to remember His holy covenant' (Luke 1:72). Here, he was speaking about God's mercies.

'And you, child, will be called the prophet of the Highest; for you will go before the face of the Lord to prepare His ways, ***to give knowledge of salvation to His people*** *by the remission of their sins'* (Luke 1:76, 77). He was prophesying about the newborn child, declaring that he would be a prophet and describing the work he would do.

We mention these highlights in order to realise how the Lord loves to see the characteristics that must be found in the faithful remnant, and how, through them, important divine purposes are fulfilled. Yet, this remnant requires a special preparation.

- ***With Elizabeth***

She declared that she had lived in reproach until the time came for her reproach to be taken away:

> *Thus the Lord has dealt with me, in the days when He looked on me, to take away my reproach among people* (Luke 1:25).

Do we believe that if we wait upon the Lord with patience and complete surrender, He will surely reward such waiting and take away our reproach? It is written:

> *The Lord God will wipe away tears from all faces, and the reproach of his people he will take away from all the earth* (Isaiah 25:8, ESV).

Also, when Mary visited her while bearing the Messiah in her womb, Elizabeth was filled with the Holy Spirit, and *'she spoke out with a loud voice and said, "Blessed are you among women, and blessed is the fruit of your womb! But why is this granted to me, that* ***the mother of my Lord*** *should come to me?"'* (Luke 1:42, 43).

Here we see her sensitive spirit and her humility, and that the Lord entrusted her to be the first one to proclaim the Messiah the Lord while He was still in the womb: *'But why is this granted to me, that* ***the mother of my Lord*** *should come to me?'*

Then, she blessed the Virgin Mary and gave us all a special beatitude—for whoever believes what the Lord says to them:

> *Blessed is she who believed, for there will be a fulfilment of those things which were told her from the Lord* (Luke 1:45).

Therefore, this man, Zacharias, who suffered greatly, was a prophet; his son was a prophet; and his wife was also a prophetess, proclaiming that the Child in the Virgin's womb was her Lord.

The Virgin Mary

She was an example of the remnant in her time.

Here, we will mention some of the characteristics and divine highlights recorded about her in order to better understand the characteristics and responsibilities of the remnant.

Her parents were Joachim and Anna. Although Scripture does not speak of them, tradition says that they had been barren, prayed earnestly, and waited for many years—yet nothing happened. Thus, they also endured reproach and pain.

Then the Virgin Mary was born. Tradition tells us that she was consecrated to the Lord from a young age and brought to the temple, where there was a place for virgins who devoted themselves to worship until a certain age, as Nazirites (Numbers 6). In this atmosphere of worship and holiness, she was being well prepared until the angel came to her with the Annunciation.

The angel said to her:

> *And behold, you will conceive in your womb and bring forth a Son, and shall call His name Jesus* (Luke 1:31).

However, the Virgin had consecrated herself to a life of celibacy, as is evident from her response to the angel: *'How can this be, since I do not know a man?'* (Luke 1:34).

The angel answered:

> *"The Holy Spirit will come upon you, and the power of the Highest will overshadow you; therefore, also, that Holy One who is to be born will be called the Son of God"* (Luke 1:35).

If we look carefully at the words, we realise that Mary did not fully understand what was happening—especially since she was not like Zacharias, who had the example of Abraham and Sarah, who had gone through a similar experience before him. Mary, however, had no precedent for such a matter in the history of Israel. Moreover, what the angel announced to her was extraordinary.

However, her spontaneous and immediate response—despite the difficulty of the situation and her lack of understanding—is remarkable. She said:

> *"Behold the maidservant of the Lord! Let it be to me according to your word"* (Luke 1:38).

What happened after that?

She went with haste to Elizabeth, because the angel had informed her about Elizabeth's pregnancy. However, her purpose in visiting was not to know or witness Elizabeth's pregnancy, but surely to share what the angel had said to her and to receive guidance from Elizabeth. For Elizabeth was the wife of a priest, and they lived a godly life, according to the Lord's commandments. Surely, their spirits were in harmony.

This young girl, who was about 16–18 years old, travelled nearly 100 miles from Nazareth, her hometown, to the hill country of Judah, where Elizabeth lived. Such a journey takes about five days on foot.

When she arrived, there was a special encounter—the outpouring of the Holy Spirit and prophetic words uttered by both Elizabeth and Mary. The Virgin Mary then proclaimed her famous song of praise, which worshipping generations have memorised and repeated from generation to generation.

> *My soul magnifies the Lord, and my spirit has rejoiced in God my Saviour ...* (Luke 1:46–56).

We notice that Mary's praise included quotations from the song of Hannah, the mother of Samuel, recorded in 1 Samuel 2:1–10. This highlights the deep relationship this young virgin had with Scripture. We also observe the words she used in her praise: *'My spirit has rejoiced in God my Saviour'*. Although she was bearing the Saviour in her womb, she still acknowledged and proclaimed her personal need for salvation.

Note: We will return later on to speak about the Virgin after giving birth to the Messiah (Luke 2).

Simeon the elder and Anna the prophetess (Luke 2:25–38):

- ***Simeon the elder***

> *And behold, there was a man in Jerusalem whose name was Simeon, and* ***this man was just and devout, waiting for the Consolation of Israel****, and* ***the Holy Spirit was upon him****. And it had been revealed to him by the Holy Spirit that he would not see death before he had seen the Lord's Christ. So he came by the Spirit into the temple. And when the parents brought in the Child Jesus, to do for Him according to the custom of the law, he took Him up in his arms and blessed God and said: "Lord, now You are letting Your servant depart in peace, according to Your word; for my eyes have seen Your salvation which You have prepared before the face of all peoples, a light to bring revelation to the Gentiles, and the glory of Your people Israel." And Joseph and His mother marvelled at those things which were spoken of Him. Then Simeon blessed them, and said to Mary His mother, "Behold, this Child is destined for the fall and rising of many in Israel, and for a sign which will be spoken against (yes, a sword will pierce through your own soul also), that the thoughts of many hearts may be revealed"* (Luke 2:25–35).

This passage speaks of Simeon the elder. Here, he is described as devout and righteous, waiting for the Consolation of Israel, and as having the Holy Spirit upon him.

He lived as a man of God, worshipping God and obeying His statutes. He had also closed his heart to the pleasures of this world and the consolations of men, because he had discovered an important truth: the Consolation of Israel.

The Consolation of Israel was the coming of the Messiah, and awaiting Him to come and accomplish the promised salvation.

Thus, he awaited the Messiah, held fast to the promises, and exercised sincere faith, yet nothing happened. When this is the state of the men of God—men of faith through whom the promises are fulfilled, as Scripture says: *'those who through faith and patience inherit the promises'* (Hebrews 6:12)—the enemy wars against them intensely.

However, the Spirit of God helped him and revealed to him a mystery. This mystery was: because of his faith, steadfastness, and trust in God's promises, his life would be prolonged until he saw the Messiah coming in the flesh. Tradition holds that his life was extended to 300 years. Whether he lived 100, 200, or 300 years, the important thing is that he completed the walk of faith.

Such a journey that extends to such an advanced age is not easy, for it is the journey of faith in God's promises. The enemy does not cease to wage war against men of faith with all his might, knowing that such people pose a great danger to him. This is because when divine promises are fulfilled, the Kingdom of God is revealed, and the kingdom of Satan—the kingdom of darkness—is exposed and condemned.

Therefore, the evil one brings repeated stabs upon men of faith, as though holding a poisonous knife to stab the heart so that faith may fail and the heart may gradually grow weak from the wounds and the bleeding resulting from these wounds.

However, the Holy Spirit brings a special consolation: the Consolation of Israel—a special gift, a form of anointing—and He heals the wounded heart. In this way, the heart acquires softness. It is as though the stabs themselves rid the heart of the hardness brought about by the Fall, and thus it becomes stronger in holding fast to the promises and remaining steadfast in faith. The hardness resulting from the Fall is the cause of doubt in those who have not acquired such softness of heart.

- ***Anna the prophetess***

Now there was one, Anna, a prophetess, the daughter of Phanuel, of the tribe of Asher. She was of a great age, and had lived with

> *a husband seven years from her virginity; and this woman was a widow of about eighty-four years, who did not depart from the temple, but served God with fastings and prayers night and day. And coming in that instant she gave thanks to the Lord, and spoke of Him to all those who looked for redemption in Jerusalem* (Luke 2:36–38).

Anna the prophetess had been widowed from a young age. She had been married for only seven years, and then her husband died. At that time, Jewish women typically married young, so it is likely that Anna was in her twenties when she lost her husband.

What a difficult trial this must have been—truly a deep and deadly wound!

It was an opportunity for the enemy to bring doubts about God and about why He would allow this. The wounded soul groans. In such circumstances, the cry of one's heart might be: "I feel as though I am dying inwardly. I wish the Lord would have mercy on me and take me to Him as well! How great the loneliness is! How heavy the days are! Everything has lost its meaning."

Yet, what happened in the midst of all this?

Amid her tears, pain, sorrow, and bitter heart, she saw the visions of God. It is written: *'The Lord knows those who are His'* (2 Timothy 2:19). Therefore, God revealed to her the deep wound in His own heart—God's heart. It is a mystical wound, manifested to us in the Crucified Christ. Yet this wound has existed since the Fall of the first man, and even before that in the divine plan, because of God's omniscience. Yes, it is a mystical, eternal wound—the very reason for salvation and the fulfilment of God's will from beginning to end. All those whom God entrusts with His purposes mystically partake in this wound.

Anna saw the wound in God's heart, and in beholding it, her own wound was healed. She turned completely towards God, worshipping Him with fasting and prayer night and day. Mysteries were revealed to her. She perceived the mystery of the Messiah who was to come for salvation, and she began to speak to others about Him. She preached of Him, drew attention to His coming, and encouraged others with the hope of His coming. A group of people began to gather around her, drawn by the radiant attraction of God's Kingdom in her. This is the group referred to as *'all those who looked for redemption in Jerusalem'* (Luke 2:38).

- ***The Virgin Mary***

She was unlike anyone else. She remained silent, listening and pondering in her heart, as Scripture says:

> *But Mary kept all these things and pondered them in her heart* (Luke 2:18, 19).

> *His mother kept all these things in her heart* (Luke 2:51).

Simeon surprised her with his prophecy and his proclamation concerning this child, Jesus, when He was brought into the temple to be presented to the Lord (Luke 2:22). He said:

> *"Behold, this Child is destined for the fall and rising of many in Israel, and for a sign which will be spoken against"* (Luke 2:34).

Then he said a personal word to her:

> *"Yes, a sword will pierce through your own soul also"* (Luke 2:35).

What is this mystical sword which the Lord permitted for His mother—the one who bore Him in her womb and would care for Him until the time of His mission?

This sword continued to pierce her heart as she witnessed the Pharisees and scribes humiliating her Son and pursuing Him, until it reached its climax—a sword that killed her from within as she saw her Son die on the cross before her very eyes.

It is the sword that carries with it a mystery of salvation for others, because the resulting suffering allows the person to partake in the mystery of Christ's suffering, making these sufferings become *redemptive sufferings.*

God chooses some human vessels and allows them to partake in these redemptive sufferings—His sufferings—for He alone is the Redeemer. This is what Apostle Paul highlights in his Epistle to the Philippians, saying: *'That I may know Him and the power of His resurrection, and the fellowship of His sufferings, being conformed to His death'* (Philippians 3:10).

Scripture refers to these vessels as *the remnant.* Their path is thorny, and their feet bleed. The doors along their journey are often closed, and some around them rejoice in their humiliation. Their path is in the likeness of the Son, the Son of God, and they mystically partake in this with Him: *'Yet it pleased the Lord to bruise Him; He has put Him to grief'* (Isaiah 53:10).

And in them, and through them, *'the pleasure of the Lord shall prosper in His hand ... By His knowledge My righteous Servant shall justify many, for He shall bear their iniquities'* (Isaiah 53:10, 11).

All these are mysteries. The Virgin Mary opened this path for us, then others followed in her footsteps. This mystery continues to work for the salvation of souls and nations!

This was the Consolation of Israel in Christ's first coming. It was a gift given to those who studied the Scriptures and focused all their energy and preoccupation on the coming of the Messiah. They were preoccupied with this matter all day long. They received this gift, and it filled their entire being. God revealed to them that the Messiah would come in their time. They obeyed God, and He granted them this gift.

And now, is anyone preoccupied with the second coming of Christ, thinking of it all day long? Without this preoccupation, we cannot receive this gift. What occupies my heart? I must empty my heart, cleanse it of everything, and fix it entirely upon the coming of Christ.

The Consolation of the Church:

What does this phrase mean, and how can we learn from it what pertains to us?

If the Consolation of Israel had rested upon *chosen vessels* in Israel, teaching them to hold on to the promises, to pray and worship day and night, and even to endure various sufferings in order to prepare the way for the Messiah—their source of consolation—what, then, is our consolation? In other words, what is *the Consolation of the Church*?

In the early centuries, the Church was of one mind, and this hope filled every heart: *Christ is coming again; let us await Him.*

They truly waited for Him day and night, living in a continual state of readiness—walking in the Spirit, worshipping the Lord, and rejoicing in His salvation.

Yet when the living hope of Christ's return and the fervent longing for His coming began to fade, the Church weakened, losing her hope, her authority, her mission, and even her holy life.

And now, are there chosen vessels who restore the Church's true and only consolation: "The Lord will return; let us await Him"? And so they await Him day and night—with love and longing, with prayer and praise, with watchfulness and the joyful acceptance of suffering—for He will come, and everything will be made new. He will reign with righteousness, and His righteousness will be proclaimed throughout the earth. Even the non-rational creation awaits Him, as though it knows that His reign will fill it with joy and gladness.

Let us listen to the Scriptures:

> *The Lord reigns; let the earth rejoice; let the multitude of isles be glad!* (Psalm 97:1).
>
> *The heavens declare His righteousness, and all the peoples see His glory* (Psalm 97:6).
>
> *For He is coming to judge the earth. With righteousness He shall judge the world, and the peoples with equity* (Psalm 98:9).

Creation awaits Him—where, then, is the awaiting of the Church?

Where are you, O Church of Christ?!

Has she wandered into a far country and made way for the spirit of the world to enter her, and thus become ignorant of the most precious thing for her, which is to await her Bridegroom, who will come and reign and grant her to partake in His reign, as a bride adorned for her husband?

Let this be our hope, our consolation, and our intercession for the Church, that she may be restored to her calling as the one holy Church, a bride for her Bridegroom, the King, Jesus Christ!

The remnant in the Epistle to the Romans:

Apostle Paul speaks of the remnant in his Epistle to the Romans, saying:

> *I say then, has God cast away His people? Certainly not! For I also am an Israelite, of the seed of Abraham, of the tribe of Benjamin.*

> *God has not cast away His people whom He foreknew. Or do you not know what the Scripture says of Elijah, how he pleads with God against Israel, saying, "Lord, they have killed Your prophets and torn down Your altars, and I alone am left, and they seek my life"? But what does the divine response say to him? "I have reserved for Myself seven thousand men who have not bowed the knee to Baal." Even so then, at this present time* ***there is a remnant*** *according to the election of grace* (Romans 11:1–5).

Here, Apostle Paul explains that the Lord did not reject Israel, and he presents evidence to support this:

1. He himself was the first proof, for he was an Israelite who was not rejected; rather, grace visited him, and he believed in Christ.
2. He refers to the days of Elijah, when the prophet thought he alone remained faithful and that all had turned away. Yet the Lord revealed to him that a remnant had been preserved despite Israel's backsliding and worshipping Baal. The ones comprising this remnant were seven thousand men who had remained faithful to the Lord, the God of Israel.
3. Then the apostle says that there was also another remnant from Israel in Paul's own time who had come to faith in Christ.
4. In every generation, there is a remnant preserved from deceit and backsliding, and who believe in Christ.
5. All these remnants have been chosen by the work of grace. In every generation of old, God saw among His people those whose hearts were faithful to Him; thus, grace visited them, and they received salvation.
6. The Apostle explains that this will continue to happen until the time of visiting Israel comes.
7. The Apostle reveals a mystery concerning this general, corporate visitation, saying:

For I do not desire, brethren, that you should be ignorant of this mystery, lest you should be wise in your own opinion, that blindness in part has happened to Israel until the fullness of the Gentiles has come in. And so ***all Israel will be saved****, as it is written: "The Deliverer will come out of Zion, and He will turn away ungodliness from Jacob; for this is My covenant with them, when I take away their sins." Concerning the gospel they are enemies for your sake, but concerning the election they are beloved for the sake of the fathers. For the gifts and the calling of God are irrevocable* (Romans 11:25–29).

III. THE CONNECTION BETWEEN CURSES AND THEIR EFFECT ON THE GENERATIONS, AND THE ROLE OF THE REMNANT WITHIN THE ECONOMY OF REDEMPTION

Let us begin by asking: Where do curses come from?

The Word of God provides the correct answer to this question. There are specific reasons why these curses happen:

1. A lack of obedience to God's commandments

'Now it shall come to pass, if you diligently obey the voice of the Lord your God, to observe carefully all His commandments which I command you today, that the Lord your God will set you high above all nations of the earth. And all these blessings shall come upon you and overtake you, because you obey the voice of the Lord your God' (Deuteronomy 28:1, 2). See also the verses that follow.

'But it shall come to pass, if you do not obey the voice of the Lord your God, to observe carefully all His commandments and His statutes which I command you today, that all these curses will come upon you and overtake you' (Deuteronomy 28:15). See also the verses that follow.

Before that, after the people of Israel came out of slavery in Egypt, the Lord commanded them to listen to Him so that they might live and go in and possess the land He had prepared for them:

> *Now, O Israel, listen to the statutes and the judgements which I teach you to observe, that you may live, and go in and possess the land which the Lord God of your fathers is giving you* (Deuteronomy 4:1).

God repeated the same command, as we read in the following chapters:

> *And Moses called all Israel, and said to them: "Hear, O Israel, the statutes and judgements which I speak in your hearing today, that you may learn them and be careful to observe them"* (Deuteronomy 5:1).

We also read:

> *Therefore hear, O Israel, and be careful to observe it, that it may be well with you, and that you may multiply greatly as the Lord God of your fathers has promised you—'a land flowing with milk and honey'* (Deuteronomy 6:3).

Thus, Israel learned God's commandments and learned to obey God, though they sometimes stumbled and failed to obey, and at other times took heed and obeyed. This continued until the time of Joshua, who led them into the Promised Land and completed for them the main battles for possessing the land. At the end of the Book of Joshua, we read the following words:

> *Israel served the Lord all the days of Joshua, and all the days of the elders who outlived Joshua, who had known all the works of the Lord which He had done for Israel* (Joshua 24:31).

However, sadly, they soon began to backslide and turn away from the Lord and from obeying His commandments. Thus, we read the following words in the Book of Judges, which records the period that followed the time of Joshua:

> *Then the Angel of the Lord came up from Gilgal to Bochim, and said: "I led you up from Egypt and brought you to the land of which I swore to your fathers; and I said, 'I will never break My covenant with you. And you shall make no covenant with the*

> *inhabitants of this land; you shall tear down their altars.'* ***But you have not obeyed My voice***" (Judges 2:1, 2).

This deviation and turning away from God continued and even increased until the time of the prophet Elijah, when Israel became completely estranged from God and even turned to pagan worship—the worship of Baal. Therefore, Elijah rebuked them so that they might awaken. We read:

> *And Elijah came to all the people, and said, "How long will you falter between two opinions? If the Lord is God, follow Him; but if Baal, follow him"* (1 Kings 18:21).

The prophet had to perform before them the miracle of calling down fire from heaven upon the burnt sacrifice in order to expose the prophets of Baal and restore Israel to their God, Yahweh. We read:

> *Now when all the people saw it, they fell on their faces; and they said, "The Lord, He is God! The Lord, He is God!"* (1 Kings 18:39).

After this great prophetic event, supported by fire from heaven, the people returned to their God. Yet this did not last long. Soon, they began to falter once again between God and the pagan gods worshipped by the neighbouring nations. There was a state of continual spiritual darkness and confusion, to which the prophet Isaiah referred, saying:

> *They do not know nor understand; for He has shut their eyes, so that they cannot see, and their hearts, so that they cannot understand. And no one considers in his heart, nor is there knowledge nor understanding to say, "I have burned half of it in the fire, yes, I have also baked bread on its coals; I have roasted meat and eaten it; and shall I make the rest of it an abomination? Shall I fall down before a block of wood?" He*

> *feeds on ashes; a deceived heart has turned him aside; and he cannot deliver his soul, nor say, "Is there not a lie in my right hand?"* (Isaiah 44:18–20).

But why are we mentioning this sequence of events concerning Israel? Some might say, "Well, this was Israel's problem, but it is not a problem we face today!"

In fact, this is something we need to pay very close attention to. Surely, we do not worship heathen gods made of stone and wood, yet our worship has also turned away from our God and Saviour, Jesus Christ, towards the worship of money, sex, and violence. These are the heathen gods of our time.

This leads us to the necessity of knowing God's purpose in calling us to obey Him and obey His commandments, and that is: to protect us from our enemies, who deceive us and ultimately lead us to actual destruction—not merely material or earthly destruction, but the destruction of our very lives here on earth. In addition, of course, to the destruction related to our eternity, for we will be found condemned before God at the time of judgement.

These enemies are the devil (externally) and the fallen human soul (internally). Our fallen soul has earthly tendencies, passions, and fleshly lusts. Our enemy, the devil, takes advantage of these matters to take hold of us and make us captive to recurring sins, destructive lusts, and corrupting habits which ultimately cause us to lose everything—our lives and purposes.

Therefore, we need to listen to the voice of the prophets in order to understand what God requests of man and the purpose for which He requests us to obey His commandments.

Let us begin with Moses. Before the people of Israel entered the Promised Land, he said to them:

And now, Israel, what does the Lord your God require of you, but to fear the Lord your God, to walk in all His ways and to love Him, to serve the Lord your God with all your heart and with all your soul, and to keep the commandments of the Lord and His statutes which I command you today ***for your good****?* (Deuteronomy 10:12, 13).

It is therefore clear that God gave man the commandments for his own good—to protect him from every evil plan that would cause his life to lose the purpose of its existence. No matter how much a person strives to fulfil his goals and dreams, he will not be able to deny the presence of a deep inner emptiness that cannot be filled by anything external, no matter what it may be. This inner emptiness continues to groan within him, preventing him from experiencing true rest and peace.

It also became evident that the person attempts to relieve his conscience through religious practices, thinking that by doing so, he pleases God and fulfils his religious duty. The Lord drew the attention of the prophets to expose such attitudes, so that people might be aware that God desires the heart, not our offerings, sacrifices, or any religious outward services. As it was in the Old Testament during the time of the old Israel, so it is in the New Testament; for man remains the same, and his inner spiritual problem has remained the same since the Fall. Its solution is found in encountering Christ the Saviour to receive the grace of salvation and eternal life in Him.

Let us listen to the Word of God, which helps us to take heed and know God's mind towards man.

In the Book of Proverbs, we read:

My son, ***give me your heart****, and let your eyes observe my ways* (Proverbs 23:26).

The prophet Micah says:

> *With what shall I come before the Lord, and bow myself before the High God? Shall I come before Him with burnt offerings, with calves a year old? Will the Lord be pleased with thousands of rams, ten thousand rivers of oil? Shall I give my firstborn for my transgression, the fruit of my body for the sin of my soul? He has shown you, O man, what is good; and what does the Lord require of you but* ***to do justly, to love mercy, and to walk humbly with your God****?* (Micah 6:6–8).

The prophet Amos also says the following words of the Lord:

> *I hate, I despise your feast days, and I do not savour your sacred assemblies. Though you offer Me burnt offerings and your grain offerings, I will not accept them, nor will I regard your fattened peace offerings. Take away from Me the noise of your songs, for I will not hear the melody of your stringed instruments. But* ***let justice run down like water, and righteousness like a mighty stream*** (Amos 5:21–24).

The Lord wants us to act justly and walk in righteousness!

Might the Lord say the same words to us when He hears our noisy singing and all the modern tools we use—musical instruments, stage lights, and noisy beats—while the singers harbour sins of lust, hatred, conflict, pride, or showing off? The Lord is unchanging, and His attitude towards man, which the prophets revealed, remains the same for every generation—whether in the Old or New Testament.

The prophet Isaiah refers to the same point, saying:

> *"To what purpose is the multitude of your sacrifices to Me?" Says the Lord. "I have had enough of burnt offerings of rams and the fat of fed cattle. I do not delight in the blood of bulls, or of lambs*

or goats ... Bring no more futile sacrifices; incense is an abomination to Me ... I cannot endure iniquity and the sacred meeting ... your appointed feasts my soul hates; they are a trouble to Me, I am weary of bearing them ... even though you make many prayers, I will not hear. Your hands are full of blood" (excerpts from Isaiah 1:11–15).

But why, Lord?

The Lord answers through the prophet, saying:

"Wash yourselves, make yourselves clean; put away the evil of your doings from before My eyes. Cease to do evil, learn to do good; seek justice, rebuke the oppressor; defend the fatherless, plead for the widow. ***Come now, and let us reason together,*** *" says the Lord, "Though your sins are like scarlet, they shall be as white as snow; though they are red like crimson, they shall be as wool"* (Isaiah 1:16–18).

This is God's heart: He invites us to reason with Him. He loves mankind and delights when we go to Him—complaining, crying out, repenting, and discovering who He is and the meaning of His commandments—so that we may fulfil the purpose of our temporary life on earth and be prepared for eternity.

The prophet Jeremiah also says the following words to the people of Israel—and to us, because we need to hear them lest we numb our consciences with religious forms or external spiritual practices while our hearts remain far from God and our conduct displeasing to Him, and lest our conduct even cause others to stumble or doubt the things of God, rather than becoming a means of salvation to those around us. Jeremiah warns, saying:

Thus says the Lord of hosts, the God of Israel: "Amend your ways and your doings, and I will cause you to dwell in this place. Do not trust in these lying words, saying, 'The temple of the Lord, the

> *temple of the Lord, the temple of the Lord are these'"* (Jeremiah 7:3, 4).

This means that we must not rely on outward forms alone. To Israel, the prophet says that the purpose is not to go to the temple and then to walk in evil. In the same way, it is as though he also says to us, as people of the New Testament: God is not pleased simply because we attend church while our conduct fails to reflect a true Christian life.

In the same chapter, the prophet goes on to highlight that God's primary request is that we listen to His voice and obey it, for in doing this is found all that delights God and all that fulfils man's purpose in life:

> *Thus says the Lord of hosts, the God of Israel: "Add your burnt offerings to your sacrifices and eat meat. For I did not speak to your fathers, or command them in the day that I brought them out of the land of Egypt, concerning burnt offerings or sacrifices. But this is what I commanded them, saying, '**Obey My voice,** and **I will be your God, and you shall be My people**. And walk in all the ways that I have commanded you, that it may be well with you'"* (Jeremiah 7:21–23).

It was necessary for us to go through this journey across the books of Scripture, because today man has replaced God's wisdom with other means he believes are more suitable for this generation. This has led to spiritual darkness and confusion, and it has become evident that Satan is the true source of the so-called wisdom our generation now embraces. Apostle James warns us directly in this regard, saying:

> *But if you have bitter envy and self-seeking in your hearts, do not boast and lie against the truth. This wisdom does not descend from above, but **is earthly, sensual, demonic** ... But the wisdom that*

is from above is first pure, then peaceable, gentle, willing to yield, full of mercy and good fruits, without partiality and without hypocrisy (James 3:14, 15, 17).

2. Evil inheritance and evil powers that work in hidden ways—the occult

To understand this important matter, we must first consider the meaning of *inheritance in earthly life*, as this will help us understand *spiritual inheritance*—whether blessed or evil—as we will explain.

A son or daughter is usually given an inheritance by their parents, who may leave them a blessed inheritance—money, property, or possessions—or leave them debts, in which case creditors may come to request payment from the children (heirs) on behalf of their parents.

The same applies to the spiritual aspect. Some parents live a life of holiness and service, which may have been handed down to them by their own parents. In this way, the spiritual blessing continues to be passed down through the generations. When a generation able to inherit the spiritual blessing arises, we may see among them spiritual leaders and people with visions for God's Kingdom who bless the whole world during their time. This is a picture of a blessed spiritual inheritance.

On the other hand, there are generations who lived in sin and evil, and this, in turn, affects their children. As a result, we may see that evil becomes imprinted on the person and dominates him to the extent that he becomes captive to it, even lacking the desire to change his life. Furthermore, if he even attempts to change, his efforts quickly fail and he is unable to persevere.

The Bible also speaks about inheritance. We have an inheritance with Christ in God. Because we have become children of God, we have been given an inheritance from our heavenly Father. We receive this inheritance through our fellowship with Christ, who has become our brother and has made us children of His Heavenly Father:

> *And if children, then heirs—heirs of God and joint heirs with Christ* (Romans 8:17).

> *Therefore you are no longer a slave but a son, and if a son, then an heir of God through Christ* (Galatians 4:7).

We can even receive an inheritance from the saints when the Holy Spirit imparts to us grace from their lives, which encourages us to walk as they walked:

> *The eyes of your understanding being enlightened; that you may know what is the hope of His calling, what are the riches of the glory of His inheritance in the saints* (Ephesians 1:18).

This is because when the saints live lives pleasing to God and according to His will, their lives become a source from which the Holy Spirit can impart grace to others. Through the example of their lives and their spiritual diligence, the Holy Spirit strengthens those who are like them and who follow in their footsteps for God's sake:

> *Remember your leaders, those who spoke to you the word of God. Consider the outcome of their way of life, and imitate their faith* (Hebrews 13:7, ESV).

All of this is good and blessed, as it reveals the blessed inheritance in its various forms. But what about the evil spiritual inheritance, whose source is the evil powers that operate in secret—the occult?

This matter often begins in a previous generation, when the head of a family faces certain problems. Then, due to being estranged from God's commandments,[8] he turns to those who are said to have spiritual authority in resolving problems, while in reality they are witches or sorcerers who operate in secret with the powers of darkness. At this point, the greatest problem begins. This is because, in biblical terms, such a person has turned away from the true God (turned his back to Him) and sought another god through the sorcerers and their evil powers. The Lord regarded this matter with great seriousness because of its danger, and therefore He had the prophet Jeremiah repeatedly warn the people about it:

> *Saying to a tree, 'You are my father,' and to a stone, 'You gave birth to me.' For they have turned their back to Me, and not their face. But in the time of their trouble they will say, 'Arise and save us'* (Jeremiah 2:27).

See also Jeremiah 7:24; 32:33.

Here, God's Word clearly reveals that in such a case, the person has replaced the true God as Father with a *'tree'*—a reference to means or objects of worshipping the devil and to works of sorcery—and God as Mother with a *'stone'*: *'Saying to a tree, "You are my father," and to a stone, "You gave birth to me"'.*

This causes a hidden evil power to sneak into the line of inheritance. It infiltrates the spiritual sphere of that person—a spiritual sphere surrounds every person and has existed since one's creation.[9] In such a case, this hidden power does not reveal itself; therefore, the person remains unaware of its presence, because it is different from the evil powers that show clear outward manifestations.

---

8 For this reason, we explained the previous point in great detail.

9 Refer to the book *The Inner Man & the Formation of Christ* by the author (Shine International Publications).

It continues from generation to generation because it considers itself the god to whom the father or grandfather of the family once turned; therefore, it also claims to be the god of his descendants. Its spiritual authority increases from generation to generation, and it becomes difficult to break its power merely by denouncing or rebuking it, because its effect would have deepened in the souls from generation to generation.

For this reason, the Scriptures reveal its nature, for it resists every attempt to break its hold, on the basis that it is a god for that person, since the person himself willingly turned to it and sought its help. As a result, it regards that person as its possession and does not wish to release its prey. Scripture says:

> *Then the Lord will bring upon you and your descendants extraordinary plagues—great and prolonged plagues—and serious and prolonged sicknesses* (Deuteronomy 28:59).

This happens because this power hides itself, while its effects in the form of prolonged sicknesses appear from generation to generation: infertility, obstacles to marriage, financial losses, lack of success in projects or in one's studies, specific illnesses that recur within the family line, and so on.

Deliverance from this evil power of the occult—whose economy is to remain hidden, as its name suggests—requires that a person return with all his heart to the true God through Jesus Christ, seeking the grace of salvation so as to live in Christ. He must then continue to persevere in faith against these sicknesses, plagues, bondages, and hindrances until they begin to break and gradually disappear. They are then replaced by blessing—the blessing of redemption to which Scripture refers when it says: '[He] *has blessed us with every spiritual blessing in the heavenly places in Christ'* (Ephesians 1:3).

This matter requires further explanation because of its importance.

An important question may arise here:

Can a curse come upon a believer in the New Testament?[10]

To answer this question, we say that Christ has lifted from us every curse—the curse of the law (Leviticus 26:14–39; Deuteronomy 28:15–63). As Scripture says:

> *Christ has redeemed us from the curse of the law, having become a curse for us (for it is written, "Cursed is everyone who hangs on a tree"), that the blessing of Abraham might come upon the Gentiles in Christ Jesus, that we might receive the promise of the Spirit through faith* (Galatians 3:13, 14).

However, this requires that the believer live a life of faith and continually walk in the Spirit.

But what if a believer has inherited such a curse from his parents, who are unbelievers?

In that case, after coming to faith in Christ, he must deal with these curses through the means granted to us in Christ's great redemption: the power of the blood of Jesus, the name of Jesus, and the Word of God.

Therefore, curses coming from previous generations do indeed affect the believer, and there is a need to discern them, as not every spiritual problem is a curse from past generations. Nevertheless, there are certain manifestations that help us discern whether it is a curse. Among these manifestations are:[11]

---

10 The words 'anathema' (ἀνάθεμα) and ‹kataraomai› (καταράομαι) occur in the New Testament. They are Greek words meaning *'curse'* or *'to curse'*. They are mentioned in Matthew 25:41; 1 Corinthians 16:22; Galatians 1:8–9; Romans 9:3; and 1 Corinthians 12:3.

11 Sometimes these manifestations are classified into six categories: defeat, disease, desolation, deprivation, deportation, and death.

- The presence of recurring sins that are difficult to overcome despite sincere spiritual diligence
- The presence of recurring sicknesses in previous generations, or deaths at an early age, whether through accidents or sudden medical conditions
- Repeated financial losses despite making every effort to avoid them
- Difficulty getting married or having children
- Persistent struggles in studies or work despite possessing strong personal and intellectual abilities

The proper way to deal with this problem includes the following:

- Proper discernment
- Repentance (including forgiving previous generations for their lack of knowledge in spiritual matters) and walking in the Spirit
- Self-examination, ensuring that there is no lack of forgiveness towards anyone, nor hatred, bitterness, anger, or psychological struggles such as self-rejection or other psychological problems that may themselves be a result of curses
- Using our spiritual weapons (Ephesians 6:10–18; 2 Corinthians 10:4, 5): praying the Psalms with prostrations and fasting, proclaiming the power of the blood of Jesus,[12] and proclaiming specific phrases against the work of sorcery or the particular kind of curse involved

There remains an important question that we should not overlook:

12 There are twelve acts of the blood of Jesus. Refer to the book *Prayers and Prophesying* by the author (Shine International Publications).

When a person who is under the authority of an evil power that works in secret comes to understand all this and sees the tragedy of his life in practice, he will most likely groan and complain, saying, "What fault is mine that I must suffer all this?"

This is, in fact, the groaning of God's own heart, for God is astonished and confused by what man does: man rejects obedience, brings all this suffering upon himself and upon his descendants, and in the end it appears as though God is the one to blame.[13]

Jeremiah speaks with God about this matter, saying:

> *O you hope of Israel, its Saviour in time of trouble, why should You be like a stranger in the land, like a traveller who turns aside to tarry for a night? **Why should You be like a man confused,** like a mighty warrior who cannot save? Yet You, O Lord, are in the midst of us, and we are called by Your name; do not leave us* (Jeremiah 14:8, 9, ESV).

God warned man beforehand, saying:

> *Keeping mercy for thousands, forgiving iniquity and transgression and sin, by no means clearing the guilty, visiting the iniquity of the fathers upon the children and the children's children to the third and the fourth generation* (Exodus 34:7).

Also, Jeremiah wrote:

'In those days they shall say no more: "The fathers have eaten sour grapes, and the children's teeth are set on edge"' (Jeremiah 31:29)—among the promises of the New Testament.

> *Our fathers sinned and are no more, but we bear their iniquities* (Lamentations 5:7).

---

13 *'The foolishness of a man twists his way, and his heart frets against the Lord'* (Proverbs 19:3).

This point is of utmost importance. Because of this evil economy—the powers that operate in hidden ways (the occult) and claim to be gods for certain people across generations—God becomes truly absent, His commandments become absent, and people become ignorant of the true God.

This is exactly what happened in the days of the prophet Elijah, as mentioned earlier. It has also happened in many ages and throughout many periods because of human evil, as people have sought other gods in various forms. In the end, the true God becomes absent, and a gap appears in history—a break from God and from the true knowledge of Him.

Therefore, a need arises to build *a spiritual bridge* that reconnects the generation that has turned away from God with an earlier time when God was known. This is the responsibility of the remnant, as we will explain later.

In fact, the remnant themselves will be this spiritual bridge through the example of their lives and fellowship with others, when they are called to teaching. Part of their responsibility is to build!

3. The heavenly places

The Bible tells us that we—believers in Jesus Christ the Saviour—have been given a new place in the heavenly places. We read:

> *And raised us up together, and made us sit together in the heavenly places in Christ Jesus* (Ephesians 2:6).

Since we have been given a place in the heavenly places, this means that we have the ability to know this place and these heavenly places. Isn't it written:

> *Call to me, and I will answer you, and I will tell you great things and inaccessible things that you have not known* (Jeremiah 33:3, LEB).

> *"Eye has not seen, nor ear heard, nor have entered into the heart of man the things which God has prepared for those who love Him." But* ***God has revealed them to us through His Spirit****. For the Spirit searches all things, yes, the deep things of God* (1 Corinthians 2:9, 10).

> *Now we have received, not the spirit of the world, but the Spirit who is from God,* ***that we might know the things that have been freely given to us by God****. These things we also speak, not in words which man's wisdom teaches but which the Holy Spirit teaches, comparing spiritual things with spiritual* (1 Corinthians 2:12, 13).

If we study the prophetic books of Scripture, accompanied by prayer and by seeking the guidance of the Holy Spirit according to the aforementioned promises, and if we become familiar with the history of the Church from its beginning and the history of the nations (or some of them), many matters related to the heavenly places that pertain to us and that we ought to know will be revealed, and we will understand our responsibility in this respect, as we will now explain.

Truths pertaining to the heavenly scene, meaning the heavenly places:

The expression *'heavenly places'* occurs in the plural form, which indicates that there are several dimensions or levels in the heavens. There are clear biblical references to this. For example, Apostle Paul speaks of Paradise as the third heaven (see 2 Corinthians 12:2, 4: *'was caught up to* ***the third heaven*** *... was* ***caught up into Paradise****'*).

- What is there in the heavenly places, or what is found in the heavenly places?
  - The believers in a spiritual state by faith (Ephesians 2:6, as mentioned earlier)

While believers still live on earth and have an actual place of presence on earth, they, at the same time, have this place in the heavens in Christ in the Spirit.

  - The various powers of darkness are also present in the heavenly places, as we read in Ephesians 6:

For we do not wrestle against flesh and blood, but against principalities, against powers, against the rulers of the darkness of this age, against spiritual hosts of wickedness ***in the heavenly places*** (Ephesians 6:12).

  - The heavenly places is also the place of the angels:

A fiery stream issued and came forth from before Him. A thousand thousands ministered to Him; ten thousand times ten thousand stood before Him. The court was seated, and the books were opened (Daniel 7:10).

See also Isaiah 6:1–3; Ezekiel 1:4–28; 1 Peter 3:22; Revelation 4:8; Revelation 5:11, 12.

- The scene in the heavenly places changed after the incarnation of Christ—with His crucifixion and resurrection—and then after the release of the apostolic work and the spread of Christianity to the whole world.

Before Christ's incarnation:

The evil spirits were dominating the heavenly places, and hence dominating the nations—being present in the heavens of these nations.

Since these evil powers had various specialities before they fell—we read about *principalities, powers, rulers,* etc.[14]—after they fell, they kept their specialties; however, instead of submitting to God's will and fulfilling His purposes in the nations, they began to submit to the evil one—the devil, the prince of the kingdom of darkness—who works in a direction that opposes God's will. His main goal is to destroy man and push him away from God, and even cause him to be offended by God and reject God, so that man may become completely captive in the hands of the evil one.

These evil powers present in the heavenly places have dominion over smaller ranks of evil spirits which are in the air, then on smaller ranks which are on the earth, and yet smaller ranks which are in man. In other words, every big evil power (principalities, powers, etc.) has smaller ranks of powers of the same kind or speciality that are spread out in the air and they operate according to the will of the bigger power. These powers that are spread in the air have further smaller and smaller extensions of their same kind, so that these small powers may be able to even invade the human soul and put evil bondages within him.

The ability of evil powers to dominate man (before salvation was completed):

- Let us look at some verses that can help us understand this point:

---

14 Ephesians 6:12; Colossians 1:16

And you He made alive, who were dead in trespasses and sins, in which you once walked ***according to the course of this world,*** *according to* ***the prince of the power of the air, the spirit who now works*** *in the sons of disobedience* (Ephesians 2:1, 2).

- Remember also that the human soul is created with great capacity and is capable of receiving many evil spirits within it when its will becomes completely corrupted and the person becomes estranged from God.

We read about this in the story of the demon-possessed man of the country of the Gadarenes:

Jesus asked him, saying, "What is your name?" And he said, "Legion," because many demons had entered him (Luke 8:30).

The number of swine into which the evil spirits entered—and which went down the steep bank into the lake and drowned—was about two thousand:

*And at once Jesus gave them permission. Then the unclean spirits went out and entered the swine (**there were about two thousand**); and the herd ran violently down the steep place into the sea, and drowned in the sea* (Mark 5:13).

- We also learn from Scripture that evil spirits present around humans in the air and on earth have various activities.

For instance, some of them are *lying spirits*:

And the Lord said, 'Who will persuade Ahab to go up, that he may fall at Ramoth Gilead?' So one spoke in this manner, and another spoke in that manner. Then a spirit came forward and stood before the Lord, and said, 'I will persuade him.' The Lord said to him, 'In what way?' So he said, 'I will go out and be ***a lying spirit*** *in the mouth of all his prophets.' And the Lord said,*

'You shall persuade him, and also prevail. Go out and do so' (1 Kings 22:20–22).

There are also *bloodthirsty spirits* to whom people offered human sacrifices in the Old Testament:

They sacrificed to demons, not to God, to gods they did not know, to new gods, new arrivals that your fathers did not fear (Deuteronomy 32:17).

They even sacrificed their sons and their daughters to demons, and shed innocent blood, the blood of their sons and daughters, whom they sacrificed to the idols of Canaan; and the land was polluted with blood (Psalm 106:37, 38).

There are also spirits that cause diseases and sicknesses, as in the case of the blind and mute man or the boy with a mute spirit (Matthew 12:22–24; Mark 9:17–29), or that cause sorrow and various kinds of uncleanness, repeatedly referred to as *'unclean spirits'* (Matthew 10:1; Luke 6:18; Acts 8:7).[15] They may come out but then return to the person if that person does not learn how to keep his deliverance (Matthew 12:43–45). There are also spirits of divination (Acts 16:16–18).

Therefore, in the history of peoples and nations, we find that some countries fell under the dominion of sorcery and witchcraft, others were characterised by widespread crime (such as murder and robbery), and others strongly resisted the faith in Christ.

From this we can understand that some curses affecting believers may sometimes result from specific evil powers that had dominated certain countries before evangelism arrived and before the gospel spread and influenced those nations. Therefore, in such cases, it is necessary to know and discern the kinds of evil

---

15 See also Mark 1:23, 26, 27; 3:11; 6:7; 7:25; 9:25; Luke 4:36; 8:29; 9:42; 11:24; Acts 5:16.

powers that dominate the heavens of the countries in which we see believers living under curses or in bondages. This will help in breaking the authority of these evil powers and freeing their captives.

After Christ's incarnation:

On the cross, Jesus put an end to the authority of the evil powers, as Apostle Paul writes in his Epistle to the Colossians:

> *Having disarmed principalities and powers, He made a public spectacle of them, triumphing over them in it* [*'it'* being the cross] (Colossians 2:15).

> *Inasmuch then as the children have partaken of flesh and blood, He Himself likewise shared in the same,* ***that through death He might destroy him who had the power of death, that is, the devil*** (Hebrews 2:14).

After the resurrection, we read in the Epistle to the Ephesians:

> *Which He worked in Christ when He raised Him from the dead and seated Him at His right hand in the heavenly places,* ***far above all*** *principality and power and might and dominion, and* ***every name*** *that is named,* ***not only in this age*** *but* ***also in that which is to come.*** *And He* ***put all things under His feet,*** *and gave Him to be head over all things to the church, which is His body, the fullness of Him who fills all in all* (Ephesians 1:20–23).

Because the nature of these evil powers is to possess and steal, they did not want to leave their places. Yet it is not the truth. They no longer possess their places in the heavens, but they are unjustly occupying them. They want to stay in the heavenly places because they do not want the believers to take these places.

However, since Christ has already disarmed these powers and authorities (Colossians 2:15), the believer should proclaim that these powers have lost their position and rank and are disarmed. He should be able to say: "This is my place; go away and leave it for me!" In this way he pushes these powers away and takes their place, which they unjustly occupy. The evil powers will try to deceive the person and make him feel that he will be unable to defeat them. However, the person should know that they are disarmed and that Christ has already completed the battle; thus, believers are only claiming the victory.

The more the believer grows in the Spirit and moves higher in his heavenly place, the more he will have *authority* over the various opposing ranks in the heavenly places. Theoretically and theologically, we have been given authority over all the powers of the devil[16] since the day we received salvation. Yet, practically, we do not have authority. Our practical authority is limited. This is why we are sometimes defeated in our warfare and are unable to help those who are bound by evil powers. However, as we take our place in the heavenly places and move up in the levels of the heavenly places, we gain practical authority over the various evil powers. In this case, it becomes a true and practical spiritual authority.

The Apostolic Age and what followed—the martyrs and worshippers:

Christianity spread throughout the world through the evangelism of the Apostles, as we read in the Book of Acts and in historical accounts.

What happened in the heavenly places as a result of this?

16 Luke 10:17–19

Faith spread, the darkness of spiritual ignorance caused by the evil powers was cast out, and the light of the gospel extended. People came to understand that idols have evil powers, that these powers deceived them, and that they had mistakenly considered the idols to be gods:

> *For all the gods of the peoples are idols, but the Lord made the heavens* (Psalm 96:5).
>
> *Let all be put to shame who serve carved images, who boast of idols. Worship Him, all you gods* (Psalm 97:7).

This resulted in the fall of these evil powers from their place in the heavenly places—the place that they had usurped since the Fall until Christ came, broke their authority, and caused them to fall.

As a result, the heavens of many countries were cleared, and these countries began to be filled with churches and believers, as the message of salvation spread mightily in them as a result of the evil powers that had dominated and blinded the minds being broken (see 2 Corinthians 4:4).

In other countries, there were mighty worshippers who, through worship in the Spirit, were able to clear the heavens over their lands, which resulted in the faith spreading powerfully in these regions. In Egypt, for example, half the population were desert worshippers, while the other half were true believers in the churches.

However, we cannot deny that there remained some other regions that opposed the gospel. It is as though the evil powers that had been broken in certain regions moved to other areas or regions to support the evil powers already present there and fortify them before the evangelists could reach those lands with the message of the gospel. As a result, these areas remained in spiritual darkness, ignorance and sorcery spread, and souls remained in bondage and spiritual captivity, as happened in some countries in Africa and Asia.

Our world today: What is the scene in the heavenly places?

Has the great spiritual scene that prevailed in the world during the Apostolic Age, then the age of the martyrs and worshippers, and then the age of missionary work and its remarkable results, remained and continued?

Unfortunately, what we see around us today provides the answer:

Many of the countries which were once pioneers and strong in Christianity, and even bore the responsibility of evangelising other nations, are no longer so. This situation has now changed, as we see in most European countries, for instance.

Similarly, in the Middle East, the ministry of the Apostles began in Jerusalem, Syria, Antioch, and the surrounding regions. In Egypt also, the monastic movement began, and the deserts were filled with worshippers empowered by the power of the Holy Spirit. Consequently, the heavens of Egypt were cleansed from the well-known curses of the Pharaohs, and the land became filled with believers and churches. However, unfortunately this situation in the Middle East changed as well!

Why? What happened?

This is a special view based on historical facts, spiritual experience, and the scenes we see in the world.

The enemy—the prince of the kingdom of darkness—saw that his kingdom was being strongly shaken and that all his dreams of dominating the world and becoming its god were endangered. He saw his soldiers falling and being replaced by praises and prayers that filled the heavenly realms. So what would he do?

He knows man and knows his weaknesses and gaps. And, unfortunately, man remains the same despite the great redemption and eternal salvation that have been offered to him. Therefore, the enemy began to observe, seize opportunities, and conspire.

Here we will present clear examples that we all know, so that they may help us wake up and perceive our responsibility as the remnant whose turn has now come to fulfil its responsibility and prepare for the second coming of Christ.

We will present two examples:

- The Middle East
- Europe

- **The First Example: The Middle East—in regions that were known for worship and holiness (Egypt, Syria, and others), faith began to weaken. Why?**

  a. The division that took place in the One Catholic Apostolic Church during the ecumenical councils in the 5th century greatly weakened the unity of the faith.

  b. The coming of Islam (7th century) brought with it certain spiritual powers.

  c. A change then occurred in the scene of the heavenly places. Instead of being filled with prayer and praise, these prayers and praises became weak and constrained. Because of the divisions mentioned earlier, the churches, pastors, and believers, instead of being devoted to worship, became preoccupied with theological disputes. They fought among themselves as fleshly attitudes, human wisdom, and the dominance of rulers began to prevail.

Then, with the Islamic occupation, the powers associated with Islam entered the heavens over these countries, as happened clearly in Egypt. These powers called upon older evil powers, the powers associated with the Pharaohs and with sorcery. As a result, spiritual darkness returned and increased, and the domineering, Pharaonic character that is filled with many evils began to prevail, even among some believers and pastors.

Divisions between the churches increased, and faith weakened. In some cases, people did not know the difference between Christianity and Islam. Political pressure on believers also increased, forcing many either to convert to Islam, face death, or pay heavy taxes that were often far beyond the ability of poor people. Thus, the situation changed completely.

This scene continued until the present time. It is true that from time to time, holy people appeared, having a messiah calling, which we will explain later in this study. There were also divine visitations from time to time.

Persecution increased, and the number of martyrs grew greatly in Egypt. Yet the blood they shed preserved the faith and became like a power interceding in heaven for the Church in that country. Without this, the Christian faith might have been completely lost, as was the case in some regions of West Africa.

Then we come to the present time. What is the situation in the heavens over this region?

The Spirit of God stirred many people from around the world to go to Egypt to intercede in various ways: groups praying all night, groups walking through the streets and praying in different provinces throughout the country from north to south, and missions that encouraged and strengthened the believers.

As a result, the power of Islamic dominion was broken, and thousands of Muslims became Christians—a matter that had never happened before, because leaving Islam and converting to Christianity meant a death sentence under Islamic law.

In my view, when these evil powers were weakened and broken through prayer, they left this region and moved into Europe. As a result, major European countries, such as France and the United Kingdom, began to embrace Islam and even serve its agenda. This happened due to the spread of spiritual darkness across Europe from the neglect of spiritual matters.

Parallel to this, other evil powers moved to the Middle East from Europe and America—powers promoting liberal morals.

Despite this painful situation, and although it has taken place on a corporate level, the Spirit of God has begun to work in an evident way among the remnant. He has begun to search for them and reveal them. Now He desires to bring them together to be strengthened and to work in order to prepare both earth and heaven for the imminent return of Christ the King. For all signs confirm that He is coming soon.

- **The Second Example: Europe**

The Enlightenment movement[17] caused the mind to take the upper hand, and thus the spirit weakened. Then the enemy devised his plan to destroy Christian morals and deceive the youth, in whom he saw an opportunity to begin his work.

Thus the well-known sexual movement of the 1970s began, and moral decadence started to spread. This paved the way for evil powers to gather, awaken the old powers, restore them once again,

---

17 This movement (18th century) robbed believers of something of utmost importance: the mystical dimension to which Apostle Paul refers in his Epistles, using the word *'mystery'*. With this movement, all spiritual matters began to be subject only to the mind. As a result, the spirit withered. Spiritual matters cannot be fully perceived by the mind, but by the spirit of a person (1 Corinthians 2:9–15).

and add to them the evil powers that came to these countries from other regions. This occurred with Islam's coinciding spread across the lands of Europe at that time, and the specific powers it brought with it. Furthermore, the powers associated with Islam that had more recently come from the Middle East, as we explained in the previous example, were added. Together, these evil powers fractured moral chastity and weakened the faithfulness, uprightness, and honesty that spring from the gospel teaching. As a result, the authority of Satan and his destruction of the youth increased, as we all know.

Important Note:

We must not forget man's responsibility within these regions and during these ages. Man bears a responsibility because the recurring sins for which he does not repent, nor therefore receive forgiveness, create evil clouds in the heavens. These clouds separate man from God and give greater opportunity for evil powers to gather together and dominate with increased authority in the heavens over these regions and countries.

Let us read what the prophet Isaiah wrote in this regard, from which we can understand that sins become like a cloud in the heavens and that repentance blots them out (herein lies man's responsibility):

> *I have blotted out, like a thick cloud, your transgressions, and* ***like a cloud, your sins*** (Isaiah 44:22).

The prophet also shows us how the iniquities create a barrier or a separation between man and God:

> *Behold, the Lord's hand is not shortened, that it cannot save; nor His ear heavy, that it cannot hear. But your iniquities have*

> ***separated you*** *from your God; and your sins have hidden His face from you, so that He will not hear* (Isaiah 59:1, 2).

Despite this, the Lord did not cease to send His Spirit with spiritual revivals that were effective, at least for some time. He also did not cease to raise up for Himself men of God who bore a special calling for such a time—a calling that we might describe as a *messianic calling*, as we will explain. They evangelised, taught, suffered, carried the yoke, and were united with Christ. Thus, His salvation worked through them, as Christ Himself worked in them. All of this happened despite the increase of evil and the expansion of Satan's authority.

It has also become clear that the Spirit of God is quickening the remnant in every place. He raises them up, prepares them, and works in them and through them, so that they too may prepare the scene of earth and heaven—each one in his place: countries, regions, and continents. For Christ is coming again, and Satan's time is drawing to an end; therefore Satan has great wrath, as his judgement is about to be manifested. The reign of Christ will come with righteousness, holiness, light, and truth, and it will fill the whole earth with rejoicing:

> *Say among the nations, "The Lord reigns; the world also is firmly established, it shall not be moved; He shall judge the peoples righteously." Let the heavens rejoice, and let the earth be glad; let the sea roar, and all its fullness; let the field be joyful, and all that is in it. Then all the trees of the woods will rejoice before the Lord. For He is coming, for He is coming to judge the earth. He shall judge the world with righteousness, and the peoples with His truth* (Psalm 96:10–13).

And now, what is the role of the remnant?

IV. OUR RESPONSIBILITY IN THIS GENERATION, AND HOW WE SHOULD VIEW THE STATE OF THE WORLD, THE CHURCH, AND THE REMNANT

We have spoken about the state of the world and the Church (believers), and now we want to explain the responsibility and role of the remnant and their work during these days in preparation for Christ's second coming. As it was before His first coming (His incarnation), so it must also be before His second coming.

A. Important concepts that we need to understand:

1. ***Is there a distinction between individuals within the remnant and their different callings? And what is the relationship between the remnant and those who have a messianic calling?***

Such questions arise from the hidden conflict and strife towards others that one may have due to the presence of unsanctified areas in the soul. They are the same conflicts that existed among Christ's disciples when they asked among themselves who was the greatest: *'Then a dispute arose among them as to which of them would be greatest'* (Luke 9:46).

However, the truth is that all the individuals of the remnant are equal in grace and spiritual honour. Each of them has undergone the stage of cleansing and suffering in order to be purified, and each has remained steadfast in their faith, abiding in Christ, and holding firmly to the great salvation. They remained steadfast even when their suffering increased and when their inner perplexity increased, raising questions such as: "Why am I in such a state? Why do I go through all these sufferings? Why are others around me different and not facing all the sufferings that I endure? What is my fault in all this?"

Yet despite all this, their hearts remained steadfast in their love for the Lord Jesus and in their trust in His mercies and His salvation. The disposition of their heart was to say with Job:

> *Though He slay me, yet will I trust Him. Even so, I will defend my own ways before Him* (Job 13:15).
>
> *Though He slay me, yet will I trust in Him: but I will maintain mine own ways before Him* (Job 13:15, KJV).

This disposition of heart—being steadfast in their love for Jesus, trusting Him, and waiting upon Him alone despite the suffering, perplexity, and the questions that seem to have no answers—approved them. Therefore, God's grace drew near to them, and His mercy preserved them and made them steadfast, so that they might be revealed as the remnant and that He might complete their preparation for the responsibility awaiting them, as we will explain shortly.

This is on the one hand; but on the other hand, each individual among the remnant has their specific calling. These callings are equally valuable. There is no distinction or difference that would create conflict. This is because a person's calling is a gift from God; the person himself possesses nothing. Also, the Holy Spirit may sometimes prepare a person for a particular calling in order to use him to carry out certain tasks. Then He may lead this same person to another calling, completing his preparation and revealing him in order to use him in other matters. The only difference among them lies in the heart: its readiness to be enlarged, its clinging to the Lord, and its burden and preoccupation with the work of God's Kingdom.

We should not forget that those who have a messianic calling are essentially part of the remnant, but have had a special journey due to certain circumstances that were all under God's control for specific purposes. We cannot understand all of God's mystical matters; yet the truth remains that these individuals do not represent a special or distinct group in any way, because everything that had taken place in their preparation was the work of God's grace. We must not make comparisons or give the enemy an opportunity to deceive us. Rather, each one must trust that he has his own calling that is equal in grace and honour. In his Second Epistle, Apostle Peter draws our attention to the truth that believers are equal in their faith, because this faith came as a gift of God.

Let us remind ourselves of the words of Scripture:

> *For by grace you have been saved through faith, **and that not of yourselves**; it is the gift of God* (Ephesians 2:8).

> *Simeon Peter, a servant and apostle of Jesus Christ, to those who have obtained **a faith of equal standing** with ours by the righteousness of our God and Saviour Jesus Christ* (2 Peter 1:1, ESV).

This means that the very faith of the Apostles is the faith of all believers. This faith bears within it the gift of each person's calling, according to how God has created him. The Lord desires that every person would have joy and delight, and He has given each one that which brings him joy and delight in fullness:

> *In Your presence is **fullness of joy**; at Your right hand are **pleasures forevermore*** (Psalm 16:11b).

2. *Another point that we need to understand is: What are the forms of the messianic calling?*

Before explaining some of these forms, let us look at two examples of this calling, one from the Old Testament and another from the New Testament.

We may be surprised by the mention of the Old Testament in relation to this calling, since it precedes the coming of the Messiah. Was there a messianic calling in the Old Testament?

Yes, because the salvific work of the Messiah extends across both testaments, for it is eternal—from everlasting to everlasting:

> *He indeed was foreordained before the foundation of the world, but was manifest in these last times for you* (1 Peter 1:20).

Therefore, the messianic work has examples in the Old Testament that manifest it.

The example we wish to mention here is that of Joseph.

Joseph was prepared through suffering, as mentioned earlier. He bore the mystery and grace of the remnant, who preserve the lives of others. Indeed, he preserved an entire generation from perishing in the famine, as we read in the story recorded in the Book of Genesis.

Let us look at some verses that show us how this human vessel was prepared for his messianic calling:

> *Joseph is a fruitful bough, a fruitful bough by a well; His branches run over the wall. The archers have bitterly grieved him, shot at him and hated him. But his bow* ***remained in strength****, and the arms of his hands were made strong by the hands of the Mighty God of Jacob (from there is the Shepherd, the Stone of Israel)* (Genesis 49:22–24).

Joseph indeed went through these sufferings. The arrows of his envious brothers shot at him and wounded him. He passed through the fire of estrangement (being a stranger in a foreign land) and even imprisonment. Yet he was strengthened because his hands held fast to the hands of the Lord, the Mighty God of Jacob, and he knew Him as the Shepherd and the Rock.

In the New Testament, we have the clear example of Apostle Paul.

Let us read about some of the suffering he endured:

> *Then the disciples took him by night and let him down through the wall in a large basket* (Acts 9:25).

This took place after he had learned that the Jews were plotting to kill him.

> *And when Saul had come to Jerusalem, he tried to join the disciples; but they were all afraid of him, and did not believe that he was a disciple* (Acts 9:26).

This is a glimpse of the rejection and mistrust that Apostle Paul faced.

He himself also mentioned a list of the sufferings that he went through, saying:

> *In labor more abundant, in stripes above measure, in prisons more frequently, in deaths often. From the Jews five times I received forty stripes minus one. Three times I was beaten with rods; once I was stoned; three times I was shipwrecked; a night and a day I have been in the deep; in journeys often, in perils of waters, in perils of robbers, in perils of my own countrymen, in perils of the Gentiles, in perils in the city, in perils in the wilderness, in perils in the sea, in perils among false brethren; in weariness and toil, in sleeplessness often, in hunger and thirst, in fastings often, in cold and nakedness—besides the other things, what comes upon me daily: my deep concern for all the churches. Who is weak, and I am not weak? Who is made to stumble, and I do not burn with indignation?* (2 Corinthians 11:23b–29).

Forms of the Messianic Calling:

- **Messiahs (the Lord's anointed)**

This means that Christ is formed within them, who carries within their hearts a burden—the burden for the salvation of souls.

Among such people were evangelists who were anointed with power, and the Lord used them to bring about spiritual revivals that resulted in the salvation of many souls.

Among them also were missionaries who went to the jungles of Africa and Asia. Many of them even offered their lives as living sacrifices, facing death at the hands of pagan inhabitants before the way was opened for the message of the gospel and the salvation of souls.

Among them also were those who interceded with tears, fasting, and prayers. Their state is best described in the words of Jeremiah:

> *Oh, that my head were waters, and my eyes a fountain of tears, that I might weep day and night for the slain of the daughter of my people!* (Jeremiah 9:1).

Yet they were also granted divine promises:

> *Thus says the Lord to* ***His anointed****, to Cyrus, whose right hand I have held—to subdue nations before him and loose the armour of kings, to open before him the double doors, so that the gates will not be shut: 'I will go before you and make the crooked places straight; I will break in pieces the gates of bronze and cut the bars of iron. I will give you the treasures of darkness and hidden riches of secret places, that you may know that I, the Lord, who call you by your name, am the God of Israel* (Isaiah 45:1–3).

They believed the promises; consequently, doors were opened before them, they were given precious souls (treasures and riches), and the Lord was with them.

- **Bearers of redemptive sufferings**

We referred earlier to redemptive sufferings and noted that those who bear such sufferings also have their own sins, weaknesses, and bondages. Yet at the same time, they have a heart that loves the Lord and is preoccupied with the matters of His Kingdom. Therefore, the Lord lays upon them some of the burdens of others—burdens of the same kind as their own sins and burdens. When the work of redemption is completed in them, their own sins are removed and their bonds are loosed. At the same time, the sins and bonds of others are also lifted, as they are laid upon those who are 'bearers of redemptive sufferings'.

Apostle Paul teaches us some truths in this regard:

In Greek, there are two words that describe the bearing of burdens that are transferred from one person to another, the bearer being a believer who is called to partake in carrying such burdens because this is how Christ has been formed within him.

The first word is *'anechomai'* (ἀνέχομαι)[18]: it refers to sharing in a burden, meaning that part of the burden is laid upon the one called to carry it.

The second word is *'bastazo'* (βαστάζω)[19]: it refers to bearing the full burden, not merely part of it, by the one called to bear it.

- References where the first word, *'anechomai'*, occurs:

Bearing *with one another in love* (Ephesians 4:2).

18 Louw Nida 25.171
19 Louw Nida 15.188

Bearing *with one another, and forgiving one another* (Colossians 3:13).

– References where the second word *'bastazo'* occurs:

We then who are strong ought ***to bear*** *with the scruples of the weak, and not to please ourselves* (Romans 15:1).

Bear *one another's burdens, and so fulfil the law of Christ* (Galatians 6:2).

- **The Image of the Lamb**

This image is characterised by meekness, heavenly attraction, and being a living testimony to the work of God's grace. This meekness results from Christ being formed within the person in the likeness of a meek lamb.

This calling leads the one who receives it to be characterised by humility, surrender to the Lord, self-denial, and the relinquishing of one's own will. Like a lamb, he accepts to do whatever is asked of him, even if it is not pleasing to him or seems beyond his ability. However, if he trusts in God's sufficient grace, he will indeed witness how this grace works in his ability, increasing and enlarging his abilities and enabling him to do all things.

Let us recall what Apostle Paul teaches in this regard:

My grace is sufficient for you, for My strength is made perfect in weakness (2 Corinthians 12:9).

I can do all things through Christ who strengthens me (Philippians 4:13).

These are some examples; yet we must not forget that everything is based on the formation of Christ within our new man (Galatians 4:19).

B. The spiritual preparation of the remnant (each individual) and those with a messianic calling

Note that those who have a messianic calling are part of the remnant, and they go through the same kind of preparation.

Yet, the particular preparation of each person corresponds to his personal calling and to the specific form of that calling, as we have just explained.

This preparation includes two main aspects:

1. Spiritual battle—primarily an inner battle
2. The building of the soul—the Lord's inner tent

Before explaining these two aspects of preparation, I would like to clarify the following:

- What is the purpose of this preparation?
- What is the picture that each person is meant to reach through this preparation?
- What happens if this picture is not reached in its fullness?

The required picture is to be conformed to the image of Christ, as Scripture says:

> *For whom He foreknew, He also predestined* ***to be conformed to the image of His Son,*** *that He might be the firstborn among many brethren* (Romans 8:29).

Yes, it is because those who will survive the judgement as the remnant (with all the various divine callings included within it) must be conformed to the image of Christ and reflect Him in their lives. Christ Himself also desires to be manifested among His brethren—those who believe in Him and perceive the greatness of the eternal salvation which He has accomplished for them, and who have earnestly obeyed the instructions of grace so that they may be filled with this salvation which transforms them into the very image of Christ.

In this way, they truly become *witnesses to the grace of salvation* to the generation that remains after the judgement and for those who will join them, so that all may perceive the greatness of salvation, obey the work of grace, and likewise be transformed to the same image—conformed to the image of Christ.

However, if some fail to reach this image that the Lord desires because they do not continue in obedience to the instructions of grace—that is, the guidance of the Holy Spirit given through their fellowship with God or through their spiritual mentors—then discrepancies will arise among the members of the remnant. While some will receive the fullness of spiritual gifts and anointing according to their calling—because they have completed their obedience and the image of Christ has been manifested in them—others will halt at a certain point in the process of sanctification. As a result, they will receive only the measure of anointing necessary to carry out part of the work, even though they had originally been called to accomplish a greater work than the one now given to them, had they completed their journey of sanctification without halting.

Now let us speak about the preparation—the spiritual battle and the building of the soul:

1. The Spiritual Battle (primarily an inner battle)

The field of this battle is the mind, that is, a person's own thoughts and convictions, and the things he holds fast to without examining them in the light of God's Word and of the guidance of spiritual mentors.

Of course, we should not forget that the remnant are believers who are advanced in grace. They have already walked a spiritual journey and have learned the principles of life in the Spirit. Yet the roots of sin in the old nature may remain and may take different forms. The most common of these forms are personal convictions, the influence of culture rooted in a person from childhood (as most likely no one would have taught him about these matters), or other influences coming from previous generations that have been imprinted on one's personality, shaping it in a particular way.

All these matters do not hinder a person's spiritual growth for a period of time, which may last quite long, until a moment comes when the person halts at a particular point in his spiritual walk. Unfortunately, this happens often.

However, if the person realises that there is yet further spiritual growth and an entrance into the glory of the children of God (Romans 8:21), he will then realise—through the guidance of the Holy Spirit—that a spiritual warfare is needed, and that the battlefield is primarily the mind: personal convictions, one's own thoughts, and cultural imprints or influences inherited from previous generations.

Then the battle begins. Its *guide* is the trustworthy Word of God:

> *And* ***do not be conformed*** *to this world, but* ***be transformed by the renewing of your mind****, that you may prove what is that good and acceptable and perfect will of God* (Romans 12:2).

Here, we find some clear points to review our lives against:

Does the form of my life bear any resemblance to the world in which I live—to my generation?

As one obeys the faithful Holy Spirit, he immediately realises that there are many matters in his life that resemble those around him—the people of this world, whether unbelievers or believers who live according to the flesh and not according to the Spirit, as Apostle Paul teaches us.

Thus, one begins his attempts to change and be skinned of these habits, imprints, and the like. Soon he perceives that the source of all these matters is the convictions of the mind that one holds on to, while they are not according to God's Word. Therefore, there is a need for transformation and for turning away from these things.[20]

As soon as the person begins his attempts at transformation, he soon finds that it is a very difficult thing. But why does he find it difficult? Because he realises that, in fact, his thoughts and convictions form a major part of his personality, or rather his whole personality. How, then, can he abandon his personality? How can he lose it? Or rather, how can he lose his very self and his sense of existence? What then would remain for him or what would he rely on if he were to let go of his character? It would mean losing oneself entirely! How can anyone accept such a loss?!

Do we not remember the words of the Lord Jesus in this regard?

> *He who finds his life will lose it, and he who loses his life for My sake will find it* (Matthew 10:39).

It is a battle of 'cutting off one's own will', as the Fathers of the Church call it. It is the battle of being transformed into the image of a lamb, so that we may truly be conformed to the image of the Lamb of God who has taken away our sins and saved us!

We cannot deny that those who have gone through this battle and completed it realised that all the powers of Hades stood against

---

20 *'For our own will is a dividing wall, separating us from God; and if it is not torn down, we cannot learn and do what accords with God's will, but are estranged from Him and tyrannized by our enemies against our will'* (St. Peter of Damascus, 11th century, The Philokalia, Volume 3).

them, for the evil powers greatly fear this transformation. For whoever becomes a lamb and is conformed to the image of the Lamb of God, Christ, the powers of evil cannot overcome him. Scripture says:

> *And this is the victory that has overcome the world—our faith* (1 John 5:4).
>
> *We know that whoever is born of God does not sin; but he who has been born of God keeps himself, and* ***the wicked one does not touch him*** (1 John 5:18).
>
> *You are of God, little children, and* ***have overcome*** *them, because He who is in you is greater than he who is in the world* (1 John 4:4).

Yes, indeed, it is an entrance into Hell in the Spirit for a time, and a completion of the spiritual battle, which Christ Himself—who dwells within us with the power of His salvation—accomplishes for us. Then, when we come out of this battle, we will have authority to deliver others from Hell.

Let us remember the words of the Lord to St. Silouan the Athonite when he entered the battle of Hell: *'Keep your mind in Hell and despair not'*. In this way, he completed his battle and came out of it, bearing the supreme teaching of the Spirit for us and for the generation.

There remains an important point to say in this context:

What can sustain the person when he enters this battle, enabling him to complete it?

What can he hold on to when he feels lost and senses the loss of everything—even his personality and convictions that he once clung to as though they were the very essence of his existence and the main characteristics of his personality?

Yes, there is one great thing, and that is *the love for Jesus*!

The more the person who enters this battle possesses a true and firmly rooted love for Jesus, the more this love becomes his sustenance, his help, and his rest, and holding on to it becomes his anchor until the battle is completed.

To conclude this point, let us remember that Jesus Himself descended to Hell and then ascended. He alone can grant a person the help needed to complete such a battle. In fact, He Himself, within the person, descends with him and then raises him up, perfected and adorned with the grace of the great salvation:

> *Now this, "He ascended"—what does it mean but that He also first descended into the lower parts of the earth? He who descended is also the One who ascended far above all the heavens,* ***that He might fill all things*** (Ephesians 4:9, 10).

Practical guidance for completing this battle:

- To have absolute surrender and trust in the hand of the Lord which guides us, according to His faithful promises:

> *I will bless the Lord who has given me counsel; my heart also instructs me in the night seasons. I have set the Lord always before me; because He is at my right hand I shall not be moved* (Psalm 16:7, 8).

> *I will instruct you and teach you in the way you should go; I will guide you with My eye* (Psalm 32:8).

> *Fear not, for I am with you; be not dismayed, for I am your God. I will strengthen you, yes, I will help you, I will uphold you with My righteous right hand* (Isaiah 41:10).

- Believe the truth of the complete spiritual way as revealed in the Word of God, and as we read in Ephesians 4:9, that all that Christ has done for our sake has become a path that we also ought to walk, if we desire to experience this great salvation.
- Recognise my need to change my mindset continually, without ceasing (for such is the problem of man), according to the commandment we have just read: *'Be transformed by the renewing of your mind'* (Romans 12:2).
- Accept suffering and humiliation, and understand their purpose, trusting that the Lord controls them while watching over us so that His full purpose may be fulfilled. Let us remember what the Word of God teaches:

> *Behold, I have refined you, but not as silver; I have tested you in the furnace of affliction* (Isaiah 48:10).

- Remember how the Scriptures describe the journey of the man of God who is prepared to be among the remnant and to enter a messianic calling (or be among the Lord's anointed), and how he is prepared in the furnace of temptations:

> *Son, when you come to the service of God, stand in justice and in fear, and prepare your soul for temptation* (Sirach 2:1, DRA).

However, we must not forget that Scripture says:

> *No temptation has overtaken you except such as is common to man; but God is faithful, who will not allow you to be tempted beyond what you are able, but with the temptation will also make the way of escape, that you may be able to bear it* (1 Corinthians 10:13).

- Read about the sufferings of the man of God who is called to these blessed matters and the different forms these sufferings take, because he is called to be a partaker of Christ's sufferings:

That I may know Him and the power of His resurrection, and the fellowship of His sufferings, being conformed to His death (Philippians 3:10).

Among the forms of suffering (that is, being a partaker of Christ's sufferings), we read:

He is despised and rejected by men, a Man of sorrows and acquainted with grief. And we hid, as it were, our faces from Him; He was despised, and we did not esteem Him (Isaiah 53:3).

Yet it pleased the Lord to bruise Him ... and the pleasure of the Lord shall prosper in His hand (Isaiah 53:10).

These verses speak about Christ Himself, as we know, and each person who is called to the messianic calling (or to the calling of the remnant according to God's will for each individual) partakes of them to a certain measure. With these sufferings there are always God's consolations, and they always yield the intended blessed fruit:

Now no chastening seems to be joyful for the present, but painful; nevertheless, afterward it yields the peaceable fruit of righteousness to those who have been trained by it (Hebrews 12:11).

Pursue peace with all people, and ***holiness****, without which* ***no one will see the Lord*** (Hebrews 12:14).

For as the sufferings of Christ abound in us, so our consolation also abounds through Christ (2 Corinthians 1:5).

2. The Building of the Soul—the Lord's Inner Tent

The building of the soul is a spiritual matter of utmost importance. In His Sermon on the Mount, Jesus teaches us, saying:

> *Therefore whoever hears these sayings of Mine, and does them, I will liken him to a wise man* ***who built his house*** *on the rock: and the rain descended, the floods came, and the winds blew and beat on that house; and it did not fall, for it was founded on the rock* (Matthew 7:24, 25).

The rock in the Scriptures refers to Christ (see, for example, 1 Corinthians 10:4).

Apostle Paul explains that the foundation is always Christ:

> *For no other foundation can anyone lay than that which is laid, which is Jesus Christ* (1 Corinthians 3:11).

But the important point is how do we build on this foundation, and what building materials do we use?

Apostle Paul goes on to say:

> *Now if anyone builds on this foundation with gold, silver, precious stones, wood, hay, straw, each one's work will become clear; for the Day will declare it, because it will be revealed by fire; and the fire will test each one's work, of what sort it is* (1 Corinthians 3:12, 13).

Here, there is a mystery that we need to understand regarding the building of our souls and how this building is to be carried out.

Let us understand this mystery step by step.

In the Old Testament, God requested that Israel prepare for Him a dwelling place, because He desired to dwell among them:

> *And let them make Me* ***a sanctuary****, that I may dwell among them* (Exodus 25:8).

At that time it was not possible for Him to dwell inside His people, because redemption had not yet been completed to restore man to fellowship with God so that God may dwell in him. We read this in the Gospel of John:

> *Jesus answered and said to him* [to one of His disciples], *"If anyone loves Me, he will keep My word; and My Father will love him, and* ***We will come to him and make Our home with him*** (John 14:23).

Notice the word *'sanctuary'*. The Lord desires to have a sanctuary within us that becomes a throne for Him to dwell in. St. Macarius the Great (4th century) writes that God created the soul as a throne for Himself (*Fifty Spiritual Homilies,* Homily 2). It is a true indwelling within the soul when a true throne is prepared within it for the Lord—a sanctuary for Him.

God has a general presence everywhere and in every person, yet He desires something more: He desires this actual indwelling within the redeemed person, because He wants to be united with him in the mystery of divine love:

> *And we have known and believed the love that God has for us. God is love, and he who abides in love abides in God,* ***and God in him*** (1 John 4:16).

But what are the features of this sanctuary, and what are its building materials?

We find the answer in the Book of Exodus, where God explained to Moses about the sanctuary that He desired His people to build for Him. What is mentioned there about the sanctuary that was to be built among the people applies to the sanctuary that is to be built within us after redemption has been completed and God's indwelling in us has become possible.

If we turn to the Book of Exodus and read the chapters that describe the tabernacle—the sanctuary built for the Lord—we find that there is an inner part for God's presence, called the Most Holy Place (see Exodus 25–27).

We notice that this part is always made of gold. In Scripture, gold refers to God's nature, according to biblical scholars.

We already know from the words of Apostle Paul—who speaks to us as a wise master builder, as he calls himself (1 Corinthians 3:10)—that there are building materials: gold, silver, and precious stones. There are also other building materials: wood, hay, and straw. In this passage, the apostle speaks about his ministry and how he builds up souls. He desires the building to be made of gold, silver, and precious stones, which means preparing a sanctuary for the Lord to dwell in them.

In the Book of Isaiah, we read how the Lord addresses Zion, which refers also to the soul, saying:

> *O you afflicted one, tossed with tempest, and not comforted, behold, I will lay your stones with colourful gems, and lay your foundations with sapphires. I will make your pinnacles of rubies, your gates of crystal, and all your walls of precious stones* (Isaiah 54:11, 12).

We also read about the city coming down from heaven—the bride of Christ:

> *Having the glory of God. Her light was like a most precious stone, like a jasper stone, clear as crystal* (Revelation 21:11).

> *The construction of its wall was of jasper; and the city was* ***pure gold****, like clear glass* (Revelation 21:18).

This is God's work in man: He transforms him into a city of gold in which He dwells. When the time comes for His coming and for the manifestation of the bride, all will appear like pure gold.

If we decide to build our souls according to this pattern, the Lord will work with us, provide us with the building materials, and transform our nature into this gold—that is, His nature:

> *By* [glory and virtue] *have been given to us exceedingly great and precious promises, that through these you may be* ***partakers of the divine nature*** (2 Peter 1:4).

Yes, everything will be tested by fire (1 Corinthians 3:13) for purification. Yet in the end, the glory of God will shine upon man—the subject of His amazing love—as Isaiah wrote concerning Zion, in a prophetic reference that extends to the redeemed person of the New Testament who has become a spiritual new Zion:

> *Arise, shine; for your light has come! And the glory of the Lord is risen upon you. For behold, the darkness shall cover the earth, and deep darkness the people; but the Lord will arise over you, and His glory will be seen upon you. The Gentiles shall come to your light, and kings to the brightness of your rising* (Isaiah 60:1–3).

Do we not see that all this has become apparent in our time and in our generation:

- Spiritual darkness covering the earth
- Spiritual darkness covering the nations
- A great deal of stumbling, confusion, and perplexity dominating everyone
- Questions without answers filling the minds and mouths of people in our generation

Therefore, there is dire need for those who are filled with the light of the Lord and upon whom His glory shines. This is the responsibility of the remnant, among other responsibilities, as we will now explain.

Our responsibility in this generation, and how we should view the state of the world, the Church, and the remnant:

We said earlier that the remnant are mainly called *to build* and *to do missionary work.*

They are preserved to carry out *an important work* under *special circumstances.* The main work is *to build,* and the special circumstances are *the desolation or destruction* resulting from judgement and all that accompanies it: wars, ruin, and tragedies.

This work also means that they are on a mission. This mission involves a broader vision than just a specific place and time—meaning, going beyond geographical or national boundaries—because it pertains to God's Kingdom, according to the Holy Spirit's revelation concerning the plan of building and the plan of expansion.

Therefore, we will discuss our responsibility in relation to the state of the world and the Church under two main aspects:

1. Building the desolations
2. Expansion—the mission

We may recall the words of the prophet Isaiah: *'And your descendants will inherit the nations, and make the desolate cities inhabited'* (Isaiah 54:3b). From these words, it is clear that there is both expansion or enlargement (*'inherit the nations'*) and building (*'make the desolate cities inhabited'*). (We will come back to this verse later.)

We need to explain this further for clarity:

1. Building the desolate places

a. The meaning of the terms,[21] according to their Hebrew origin:

- Desolate/desolation

It includes:

- – Actual, physical desolation of places: ruined homes, aftermath of fires, and the deterioration in the economic, educational, and health conditions of communities or societies
- – Geographical desolation that alters the boundaries of cities and regions
- – Psychological or emotional desolation: a sense of despair and loss
- – Desolation that brings a sense of loneliness, fear, and the destruction of everything, along with the impact of all this on the lives of believers

- To build /banah/ (בָנָה)

Restoring and stabilising all things:

- – Identity and vision
- – Relationships
- – Society and its conditions: economically, educationally, and in terms of healthcare
- – The impact of this on the Church, as believers are part of society

21 According to TDOT (Theological Dictionary of the Old Testament) and DBL (Dictionary of Biblical Language)

b. Specifying the tasks of building

This includes:

- Identity and vision
- Correcting misconceptions
- Inner building of the soul

Identity and vision

Changing the mindset: Rather than seeing this remnant as a product of past ruin, or as the generation of young people often described as "lost" or "broken", the reality is the opposite—they are a generation of building and vision.

Therefore, the first task of building begins within the remnant themselves, ensuring that they understand their position as those who were preserved and called to new tasks and a future vision—one that includes both them and their countries and churches.

Correcting misconceptions

This will inevitably collide with some incorrect or incomplete concepts, as well as questions that need answers. One of the most important of these misconceptions is the question we referred to earlier: "What is my fault, that I have had to go through all these tragedies?" Even though I was saved and the Lord preserved me, deep within I feel pain, wounds, and confusion as I compare myself with those around me and ask: "Why did all this happen to me?" In fact, what I went through has left me with wounds, pain, and fears.

Now, it is time to answer this important question: What is my fault? Why did this happen?

The Lord did not desire for this to happen to me at all. Rather, it is man's free will that has chosen not to obey God's commandments. Over many generations, man caused God to be completely absent, and no one cared for Him or sought Him. Everyone wanted to live for themselves, and some even doubted the existence of God—just as happened in the days of Elijah and continues to happen from time to time.

Yet the time of divine visitation comes, as it did during Elijah's time or at the time of the Flood before that. The Lord waits and waits, and when evil increases, something significant occurs: God becomes absent, and a break or separation takes place in man's relationship with Him. This means a break occurs in the history of God with man. Dealing with this break requires *building a bridge* in order to restore this relationship and to restore God to humanity once again. This is the work of the remnant.

First, God reveals His secrets to them: *'The secret of the Lord is with those who fear Him, and He will show them His covenant'* (Psalm 25:14). This truly happens because the Holy Spirit, who has preserved this remnant according to the divine economy, knows that they need this understanding. He reveals His secrets and teaches them Himself: *'He will teach you all things'* (John 14:26); *'He will guide you into all truth'* (John 16:13).

Yes, He has preserved them because they remained steadfast in their love for the Lord and held fast to Him despite their inner pain and the unanswered and confusing questions. Now, the Spirit of God comes to answer their questions and to teach them. He reveals these matters to them and thus helps them understand that He will work with them to build *this bridge,* and that all their pain will be healed and even transformed into ornaments[22] and glory:

---

22 The ornaments adorn the bride as part of the process of her preparation (Song of Solomon 1:10–11).

> *But rejoice* ***to the extent that you partake of Christ's sufferings****, that when His glory is revealed, you may also be glad with exceeding joy. If you are reproached for the name of Christ, blessed are you, for the* ***Spirit of glory and of God rests upon you****. On their part He is blasphemed, but on your part He is glorified* (1 Peter 4:13, 14).

When the Holy Spirit reveals this to them, they realise how much more privileged they are than others in their generation. The groaning, "What fault is mine?", is then replaced with a song in their hearts: "What glory! What joy! Blessed am I! Glory to You, O Lord!"

And now, after these misconceptions have been corrected, they begin, with energy, zeal, and confidence, to work with the Spirit of God to build—to rebuild the desolations: the desolations of souls, which inevitably are reflected in society and the Church.

Inner building of the soul

We have already explained this point when discussing the preparation of the remnant. You may refer back to that section, since the building of the soul is the same for everyone—whether for the remnant or for those living through times of judgement and desolation.

This inner building means building the inner tent of the Lord, so that we may be prepared for His indwelling within us.

c. The richness of salvation and the greatness of redemption

Now, the remnant have realised their responsibility and the work they must do: to correct misconceptions, to build the bridge that reconnects generations with one another and with God, and to build up the souls of those they encounter, for whom they become responsible.

However, this work of building amid such circumstances is not easy. Therefore, there is a need to discover the riches of grace and the greatness of salvation, which have become absent from the generations because of the break that has occurred in man's relationship with God. Now there is a need for further divine revelation, supported by the authority of the powerful anointing of the Holy Spirit, to teach the truths of salvation to this generation and help them experience these truths. This is what will build souls and build the bridge, and through this the true God will be revealed—the Lover of mankind, whose works are marvellous and who is full of wisdom and glory:

> *I will praise You, O Lord, with my whole heart; I will tell of all* ***Your marvellous works****. I will be glad and rejoice in You; I will sing praise to Your name, O Most High* (Psalm 9:1, 2).

> *O Lord, You are my God. I will exalt You, I will praise Your name, for* ***You have done wonderful things****; Your counsels of old are faithfulness and truth* (Isaiah 25:1).

> *"Behold, God is my salvation, I will trust and not be afraid; 'For Yah, the Lord, is my strength and song; He also has become my salvation.'" Therefore with joy you will draw water from the wells of salvation. And in that day you will say: "Praise the Lord, call upon His name; declare His deeds among the peoples, make mention that His name is exalted. Sing to the Lord, for He has done excellent things; this is known in all the earth"* (Isaiah 12:2–5).

This leads us to explain our new heavenly position in Christ Jesus and what it means to worship in spirit and in truth:

This must first be perceived and experienced by the remnant, who witness its great effect; then they teach it to their generation. In this way, the Church enters her true place in the heavenly realms, and her unity with Christ the Head reveals the reality of her authority and mission.

- The new heavenly place

We know that through His resurrection, Christ has granted a new heavenly place to those who believe in Him:

> *And raised us up together, and made us sit together in the heavenly places in Christ Jesus* (Ephesians 2:6).

The remnant—with all its various callings, such as the messianic calling, the Lord's anointed, and the bearers of redemptive suffering—discovers its new place, begins to abide in it, and works from it. Thus, they experience the spiritual authority through which the matters of God's Kingdom are truly accomplished. Things begin to change: the lives of the people they serve, as well as the heavenly scene of their nations. The remnant is now able to discern this scene in the heavens and perceive God's will concerning it. Through fellowship with the Holy Spirit, this scene is transformed according to God's will. In this way, the lives of individuals are transformed, and even the state of the nations is transformed!

- Worship in spirit and truth

In the Gospel of John, we read the words of Jesus:

> *God is Spirit, and those who worship Him must worship in spirit and truth* (John 4:24).

How can this be achieved?

To understand this practically and live it out as the remnant—and thus be able to teach it while building up souls in this task of building—we need to bring these truths together:

And raised us up together, and made us sit together ***in the heavenly places in Christ Jesus*** (Ephesians 2:6).

Must worship in spirit and truth (John 4:24).

First, notice the phrases:

- In the heavenly places
- In Christ Jesus

In the heavenly places:

After the Fall, the heavens were closed—it was as though firmly closed. Then Christ tore them open. When did this happen? At the Jordan, and then at the cross. The Gospel of Mark (1:10) says *'the heavens being torn open'* (ESV), or 'split apart' (LEB), or 'parted' (NKJV)—unlike the Gospels of Matthew and Luke, which simply say that 'the heavens were opened'. The expression *'torn open'* reveals that the heavens had been firmly closed.

Then, when Christ was incarnate and appeared at the Jordan River as the new Adam—the Second Adam—the Holy Spirit, who had been, as it were, separated from man since the Fall and had longed to return to man, saw Him. As soon as He saw Him, He quickly tore open the heavens and rested on Him.

The opening of the heavens began at the Jordan and was established at the cross, when redemption was accomplished.[23] We read this also in the Epistle to the Hebrews:

Therefore, brethren, having boldness to enter the Holiest ***by the blood of Jesus,*** *by a new and living way which He consecrated for us, through the veil, that is, His flesh* (Hebrews 10:19, 20).

23 John 19:30

It is granted to every believer to have open heavens continually and to have a living way through the work of the shed blood—the blood of Jesus, which remains living, as though it never ceases to flow and does not clot.

However, at times, our fleshly conduct leads to sin. These sins can become like clouds that cover the open heavens. We must discern this and live in continual repentance, so that our heavens may remain open. In this way, we remain in the heavenly places at all times.

Yet, why does the apostle continue the sentence with the phrase '*in Christ Jesus*'? Is it not sufficient to stop at the phrase: '*in the heavenly places*'?

In fact, the apostle explains this in the same epistle, in the preceding chapter:

> *Which He worked in Christ when He raised Him from the dead and seated Him at His right hand in the heavenly places, far above all principality and power and might and dominion, and every name that is named, not only in this age but also in that which is to come. And He put all things under His feet, and gave Him to be head over all things to the church, which is His body, the fullness of Him who fills all in all* (Ephesians 1:20–23).

It is of utmost importance to understand the status of Jesus after the resurrection according to the divine economy:

- All things are put under His feet
- All evil powers, with all their ranks, are under His feet
- Evil people are under His feet
- Governments and all temporal secular authorities are under His feet

This does not mean that Christ acquired something new for Himself after the resurrection, for He is God, one in essence with the Father, and He already possessed all this authority. Rather, what has changed after the resurrection relates to the flesh through which He died and rose again. Thus, this body has acquired all this authority. The body is the Church, if she is truly and actually united with the Head. Christ has lifted her above all these powers so that she may become a source of inspiration and guidance—even to secular authorities, whether believers or unbelievers. This has indeed happened, and continues to happen, in different parts of the world throughout various ages.

Now, how do we understand the phrase 'worship in spirit and truth'?

Yes, this is another aspect that complements what we have just explained and helps us understand the practical side, so that we may worship in spirit and in truth.

A believer may perceive one aspect (being in the heavenly places) but may not be aware of the other aspect (being in Christ Jesus), and therefore may not understand the intended meaning of the phrase *'worship in spirit and truth'*.

It actually means that one may perceive that he is a member in the body of Christ yet remain disconnected from the Head. As a result, there will be times when one suffers from the strikes of the evil one and of evil people, leading to consequences such as weakened faith, hindered spiritual steps, and a diminished ability to discern the fullness of God's will.

Therefore, I must perceive the full truth (worship in spirit and in truth), which means remaining always in the body and being aware of its connection to the Head.

Practically, this requires paying attention to the following:

- My state
- My mindset
- My spiritual circle—those around me

My state

Fluctuating between living according to the flesh and living according to the Spirit is a sign of spiritual immaturity—the phase of spiritual childhood. There is a need to grow into maturity in order to become true men of God and to remain steadfast in walking in the Spirit.

My mindset

We must be vigilant in continually renewing our minds:

> *And do not be conformed to this world, but be transformed by the renewing of your mind, that you may prove what is that good and acceptable and perfect will of God* (Romans 12:2).

Without the continual renewal of my mind, I will not discern the good, acceptable, and perfect will of God; consequently, discovering God's calling for me personally will be hindered.

My spiritual circle

As for people of the world, it is natural to exercise discernment and reservation towards them, since I am set apart for the Lord (2 Corinthians 6:14–7:1). However, among believers, it is truly sad when I find that I love some, hate others, reject some, or think evil of others. All this constitutes a breaking of the commandments. A man of God must maintain a pure conscience and a pure heart towards all.

The remnant perceive all these matters and are trained in them. Consequently, their ministry of building up souls—entrusted to them—becomes a work carried out in spirit and in truth. They learn to worship in spirit and in truth and to take their place in the heavenly places. This will inevitably have an impact on the Church, society, and the world!

2. Expansion—the mission

Enlarge the place of your tent (Isaiah 54:2).

In this chapter (54), we see a complete picture of an example of the remnant, particularly as a messianic calling or the calling of the Lord's anointed. Therefore, we want to highlight some important features from it that relate to our topic of the remnant, especially the aspect of expansion or broadening.

In this chapter, the prophet Isaiah presents an image of a barren woman who has gone through various stages of chastening in preparation for her calling. He describes her as *'a woman forsaken and grieved in spirit'* and as *'a youthful wife when* [she was] *refused'* (verse 6).

Imagine a young bride whose husband has rejected her. Thus, her days have become filled with sorrow and she has become forsaken. Imagine how others might point at her, making various condemning remarks—suggesting that she may have sinned, that she is barren because a curse is upon her, that she did not know how to honour her husband and was therefore rejected, or other similar hurtful comments.

Even more than that, a time came when she felt as though the Lord Himself had forsaken her:

For a mere moment I have forsaken you (verse 7).

> *With a little wrath I hid My face from you for a moment* (verse 8).

What is all this, Lord? It is very difficult! How can a human soul bear such pain?!

Yet it is the Lord's amazing grace that sustains the soul in times of suffering and throughout the process of preparation. Then we see how great what the Lord has prepared for her is when the time comes for the manifestation of her calling:

> *Sing, O barren ... Break forth into singing ... For more are the children of the desolate than the children of the married woman* (verse 1).

'*Enlarge the place of your tent*' (verse 2). (We will come back to this verse because it is directly related to our discussion about expansion and enlargement.)

> *Do not fear, for you will not be ashamed; neither be disgraced, for you will not be put to shame; for you will forget the shame of your youth* (verse 4).

> *With great mercies I will gather you* (verse 7).

> *With everlasting kindness I will have mercy on you* (verse 8).

> *My kindness shall not depart from you, nor shall My covenant of peace be removed* (verse 10).

This is what happens with God's special calling for the remnant, according to the various forms of callings within it, as explained earlier.

Now we will focus our discussion on expansion:

> ***Enlarge*** *the place of your tent ... you shall expand* ***to the right and to the left*** (verses 2, 3).

Let us first begin by understanding the meaning of the word *'enlarge'* according to the Hebrew origin:

Is it merely a geographical expansion?

In fact, it is not. Rather, it refers to an expansion or broadening that includes personality, identity, relationships, and human capacities, as seen in the way the word is used (in Hebrew) in various books of Scripture in the Old Testament.

The word *enlarge* comes from the Hebrew root *'rahab'* (בָּחָר), meaning *to open oneself wide.*[24]

Examples of the use of this word in the Old Testament:

- *And Hannah prayed, and said, My heart rejoiceth in the Lord, mine horn is exalted in the Lord:* ***my mouth is enlarged*** *over mine enemies; because I rejoice in Thy salvation* (1 Samuel 2:1, KJV).

Hannah the prophetess, Samuel's mother, speaks of her mouth being enlarged over her enemies, referring to her victory over those who had previously "enlarged their mouths" against her by humiliating her: *'And her rival also provoked her severely, to make her miserable, because the Lord had closed her womb'* (1 Samuel 1:6).

- *Hear me when I call, O God of my righteousness:* ***Thou hast enlarged me*** *when I was in distress; have mercy upon me, and hear my prayer* (Psalm 4:1, KJV).

Here the Psalmist explains that his soul was distressed because of difficult circumstances that surrounded and constrained him; yet he sought the Lord, and the Lord relieved his distress—enlarging and broadening him in the midst of it.

24 BDB (Enhanced Brown-Driver-Briggs Hebrew and English Lexicon)

- *Thou hast* ***enlarged my steps*** *under me, that my feet did not slip* (Psalm 18:36, KJV).

Here the Psalmist uses the word *'enlarged'* to indicate that his feet became firm and that he could walk quickly without slipping.

- *I am the Lord your God, who brought you out of the land of Egypt;* ***open your mouth wide****, and I will fill it* (Psalm 81:10).

Here the Psalmist refers to the Lord who invites him to open his mouth wide, promising that He will fill it according to his need. *'Enlarge'* is used here in relation to the mouth—whether to receive boldness in speech, to be given wisdom, or to ask for any need.

- *I will run the course of Your commandments, for You shall* ***enlarge my heart*** (Psalm 119:32).

Here the heart is described as being enlarged when a person carefully and continually obeys God's commandments (*'run'*). There is also a similar reference to the enlargement of the heart in Isaiah 60:5.

- *He* ***enlarges*** *his desire as hell* (Habakkuk 2:5).

This presents a negative picture in which the soul is enlarged for evil purposes.

All the above verses clarify that, in its original Hebrew usage, the word carries far more meaning than mere geographical expansion. Rather, expansion here encompasses all aspects of the personality and its circumstances.

The question now is: how can this be practically achieved?

- Trusting God's promises

As we have seen in Isaiah 54, God allows chastening and suffering for the sake of one's preparation for their calling. Yet, in all this, there are always promises which sustain the person who passes through suffering until it fulfils its purpose. Then the person comes out strengthened by the Spirit of God, and the arm of the Lord works with them. Consequently, doors are opened for this person to correct the misconceptions of the generation and rebuild the desolations of souls, because the arm of the Lord works with him. All this is included among God's promises:

> *Fear not, for I am with you; be not dismayed, for I am your God. I will strengthen you, yes, I will help you, I will uphold you with My righteous right hand* (Isaiah 41:10).

> *For I, the Lord your God, will hold your right hand, saying to you, 'Fear not, I will help you'* (Isaiah 41:13).

> *Behold, I will make you into a new threshing sledge with sharp teeth; you shall thresh the mountains and beat them small, and make the hills like chaff. You shall winnow them, the wind shall carry them away, and the whirlwind shall scatter them; you shall rejoice in the Lord, and glory in the Holy One of Israel* (Isaiah 41:15, 16).

> *Thus says the Lord* ***to His anointed****, to Cyrus,* ***whose right hand I have held****—to subdue nations before him and loose the armour of kings, to open before him the double doors, so that* ***the gates will not be shut****: '****I will go before you*** *and make the crooked places straight; I will break in pieces the gates of bronze and cut the bars of iron. I will give you the treasures of darkness and hidden riches of secret places'* (Isaiah 45:1–3a).

These are true promises of God for those who believe them. It is the Lord who works in us for His good pleasure and to fulfil His will. He only asks that we believe His promises so that we may truly receive them.

- Forming small groups or units

When we spoke about Anna the prophetess in the context of presenting the Child Jesus in the temple (Luke 2:36–38), we saw how the example of her life and her sharing with others most likely led to the formation of groups that understood God's purpose at that time—the time of the incarnation. These groups also waited, together with Anna, for the coming of the Messiah: *'She gave thanks to the Lord, and* ***spoke of Him to all those who looked for redemption in Jerusalem'*** (Luke 2:38).

We need to speak, explain, and testify, trusting that God will bring into our path those prepared souls whom the Spirit of God has already prepared. In this way, they will quickly believe our testimony and join us in waiting for the second coming of Christ to reign, as the Scriptures testify.

These groups may require further clarification through teaching, explanation, and discipleship, so that they may understand that the Lord actually desires us to prepare a sanctuary for Him to dwell among us. In this way, He Himself will fulfil the purposes of the end times (our present time) as He works with us and in our midst.

These groups are what we call *New Zion units.*[25]

- We also need to learn to have a vision for the work of God's Kingdom, based on His promises and His economy for the consummation of salvation.

We know that all the nations of the world must return to the Lord and believe in Him, as Scripture says:

25 For a detailed explanation of this topic, refer to the book *Zion: A Scriptural Study & A Vision of Ministry* (Shine International Publications).

All the ends of the world shall remember and turn to the Lord, and all the families of the nations shall worship before You. For the Kingdom is the Lord's, and He rules over the nations (Psalm 22:27, 28).

We ought to have a vision for the work that the Lord has commissioned us to do, and this vision must be aligned with this promise (Psalm 22:27–28).

We can learn this matter from the ministry of Apostle Paul:

While he was in Asia, he purposed in his heart that after leaving Asia, he would go to Jerusalem to attend Pentecost, and then go on to Rome, the capital of the Roman Empire, which was the centre of the world at that time (Acts 19–20).

When these things were accomplished, Paul purposed in the Spirit, when he had passed through Macedonia and Achaia, to go to Jerusalem, saying, "After I have been there, I must also see Rome" (Acts 19:21).

And what he purposed actually came to pass.

He was confronted by evil powers, opposing authorities, and various circumstances, and in the end, he was imprisoned in Jerusalem and then sent in chains to Caesarea. He suffered greatly, yet the Lord appeared to him and said, *'Be of good cheer, Paul; for as you have testified for Me in Jerusalem, so you must also bear witness at Rome'* (Acts 23:11).

Do we believe?

The apostle arrived in Rome despite the warnings of those who loved him, who urged him not to go to Jerusalem because he would be bound there, according to prophecies proclaimed concerning him:

> *And as we stayed many days, a certain prophet named Agabus came down from Judea. When he had come to us, he took Paul's belt, bound his own hands and feet, and said, "Thus says the Holy Spirit, 'So shall the Jews at Jerusalem bind the man who owns this belt, and deliver him into the hands of the Gentiles.'" Now when we heard these things, both we and those from that place pleaded with him not to go up to Jerusalem. Then Paul answered, "What do you mean by weeping and breaking my heart? For I am ready not only to be bound, but also to die at Jerusalem for the name of the Lord Jesus." So when he would not be persuaded, we ceased, saying, "The will of the Lord be done"* (Acts 21:10–14).

Yes, as the apostle desired, so it came to pass. He finally arrived in Rome, yet he arrived bound in chains for the sake of the gospel!

Despite his chains, he was able to serve freely for two whole years, as we read towards the end of the Book of Acts:

> *Then Paul dwelt* ***two whole years*** *in his own rented house, and received all who came to him, preaching the Kingdom of God and teaching the things which concern the Lord Jesus Christ with all confidence, no one forbidding him* (Acts 28:30, 31).

Finally:

The most important thing is to have a heart that is in harmony with God's heart, so that it may perceive the mysteries of the Kingdom of God and discern His timing in His work, and begin to learn how to work with Him in fellowship with the Holy Spirit, just as He worked with the Apostle Paul:

> *We then, as workers together with Him* (with God) *also plead with you not to receive the grace of God in vain. For He says: "In an acceptable time I have heard you, and in the day of salvation*

I have helped you." Behold, now is the accepted time; behold, now is the day of salvation (2 Corinthians 6:1, 2).

Do we accept this picture?

Do we believe?

Come, let us work with God!

For He who worked in times past with the great apostle to the nations still desires to work with us now—in our generation and at this present time!

Amen

Made in the USA
Coppell, TX
27 May 2026

77838586R00090